Vegan Tapas

M000267272

Also by Julia Barnard

Vegetarian Tapas: 150 quick and delicious snacks and bites for sharing

Promoting Happiness: a workbook to help you appreciate and get the most out of your life

50 Ways to Increase Your Happiness

How to be Happy: a collection of 60 happiness writings

Make the Change: over 250 tips for your wellbeing and happiness

Online Counselling: a guide for therapists

Vegan Tapas

150 quick and delicious snacks
& bites for sharing

Julia Barnard

© Julia Barnard 2015

First Published 2015 in Australia

Except as provided by the Copyright Act 1968 of Australia, no part of this publication may be reproduced, stored in a retrieval system or transmitted in any form or by any means without the prior written permission of the publisher.

MTC Books
PO Box 356
McLaren Vale
SA 5171
Australia
books@makethechange.com.au

National Library of Australia Cataloguing-in-Publication entry:

Creator:	Barnard, Julia, author.
Title:	Vegan tapas : 150 quick and delicious snacks and bites for sharing / Julia Barnard.
ISBN:	9780980759075 (paperback)
Notes:	Includes index.
Subjects:	Tapas.
	Appetizers.
	Snack foods.
	Vegan cooking.
	Vegetarian cooking.
Dewey Number:	641.5636

ISBN 978-0-9807590-7-5

Cover design by Pandelaide

http://veggietapas.com

Contents

Introduction

Welcome to Vegan Tapas! I am excited to be bringing you this collection of recipes perfect for sharing.

The term 'tapas' originates in Spain and is thought to mean 'to cover' and may stem back to when drink was covered with a piece of bread or meat. These days, bars in Spain serve up tapas along with drinks and popular tapas choices include olives, tortilla and patatas bravas. Tapas restaurants have cropped up all over the world. If you have ever visited a tapas restaurant you will know that the food in them is varied and no longer just features Spanish classics. The term 'tapas' has come to be synonymous with 'food for sharing'. And food for sharing is the theme of Vegan Tapas.

The recipes featured here need not be used exclusively for a tapas party. In fact you may wonder if *Tomato and Mustard Quiches* and *Treacle Tarts* even belong at a tapas party. However, all the foods here are perfect for sharing, whether it is for tapas, meze, buffets or picnics. You may want to quickly produce a few snacks for when friends come over for the evening. Or perhaps something to nibble on in front of the television. There are options for all of these occasions.

In compiling these recipes I wanted to ensure you would not have to be wandering the streets in search of some obscure ingredient. I hope you will be able to get most of your ingredients from your local supermarket, leaving you time to cook and eat. I also wanted the recipes to be easy to prepare. However, I hope you have the opportunity to try new things – develop new skills and try new flavour combinations.

If you are having a tapas party, you may be wondering how best to manage it. To try and help you out, you will notice that at the end of each recipe I tell you the quantity. This way you can calculate how well each recipe will suit your needs. You will want to consider how many guests you will be entertaining, whether the food is the sole focus of your party and whether you are serving up the dishes all at once or one at a time. You may even like to bring out a couple of different dishes at a time. This is all up to you. It's your party, so you get to make the rules.

Whether you are having a tapas night or a buffet, try to seek out a variety of serving bowls, dishes and platters. There is an enormous range out there; small dishes to serve up dips, nuts and olives and gorgeous platters for your arrangement of desserts.

I have broken the book down into nine chapters, beginning with **Dips**. One of the most sociable ways of eating is to provide a selection of dips and some wonderful snacks for dipping in them. Having created some flavoursome dips, it can sometimes be a struggle to find suitable accompaniments. Scattered throughout the book are recipes that are perfect for dipping. To make things easy for you, I have listed them at the start of the chapter for easy reference. As you will notice, you will not be short on ideas.

The next chapter is **Toppings**. It may seem strange having a chapter called toppings, but bear with me. The idea behind this chapter is to provide you with a variety of recipes that can be used as a topping. Rather than limiting your choices, I want you to be able to mix and match recipes. As with the dips chapter I have made things easy for you by listing those snacks that demand to be topped.

You will obviously find vegetables scattered throughout other chapters, however in the third chapter **Vegetables**, the focus is on the vegetable itself. Most of these recipes are quick to prepare. The *Squashed Squash* will require the most time, but not too much effort. You roast the squash in the oven, allowing you to get on with other tasks. If you are in a super hurry, put together some *Crudités* with a couple of dips. The recipe I am happiest with in this chapter has to be *Eggplant Bites*. I don't really like eggplant, but I do like these.

Chapter four is **Tofu and 'Cheese'**. Tofu is such a versatile ingredient and has been used in a variety of ways in this chapter. As you would expect from a tapas cookbook, you will find a vegan version of *Classic Tortilla* as well as a couple of variations on this simple dish. Many of the tofu recipes require draining the tofu to ensure you get a good result. I have explained how to do this in *Cook's Notes*. Some also require marinating, so make sure to leave time for this. The chapter ends with two vegan cheese recipes: *Parmesan-style Wafers* and *Crumbed 'Cheeses'*. Use your preferred brand of vegan cheese, although I used *Cheezly* for great results.

Grains, Pulses and Nuts make up the next chapter. I have included a few stuffed vegetables recipes that use couscous, rice and bulghar wheat. Feel free to vary these grains. Barley, spelt and quinoa would all work well. I have made sure none of the pulses used in the recipes need pre-soaking; I'm never that organised and the canned variety works just as well. For a quick TV snack you may enjoy the *Spiced Chickpeas* as well as *Herby Nuts* and *Spicy Roasted Nuts*.

Next there is a whole chapter dedicated to **Potatoes**. Potatoes are so versatile and make a perfect snack for sharing. If you are a fan of garlic do try

Potatoes in Garlic Sauce. Crispy potatoes smothered in an easy to prepare creamy garlic sauce. Fantastic. Make sure to try the *Sweet Potato Fries, Spiced Potato Wedges* and *Crispy Baked Potato Skins.* They are all oven-baked and far superior to anything you will find in the freezer and really quick to prepare. You will also find a vegan Scotch egg here. Since they only look like Scotch eggs, I've called the recipe *Let's Call Them Scotch Eggs*.

Chapter seven is **Bread, Polenta and Fritters**. *Bruschetta, Crostini* and *Melba Toast* make perfect bases for topping. As well as recipes to make your own *Spiced Flatbread* and *Grissini*, you also get to jazz up ready-made tortillas and pita breads with a mixture of spices. Polenta is the ideal accompaniment to toppings and dips. You will need to allow time to firm up the polenta in the fridge before grilling. The chapter ends with *Blini*, which are a pancake rather than a fritter but are great for entertaining so had to be included here.

Pastries and Biscuits follows. For all the pastry recipes I have used ready-made pastry. It will save you lots of time, allowing you to focus on the flavours. My favourite recipe has to be *Herby Tomato Tarts;* so quick yet the flavour is sublime. I have avoided filo for the *Spanakopita*, using wanton wrappers instead. I always seem to have filo left over whenever I work with it and it falls apart way too easily for my liking. Wanton wrappers resolves this, and they do taste good.

I've always been a fan of saving the best until last and this is definitely true here. Chapter nine is **Desserts**. You will find 20 recipes for those with a sweet tooth. *Churros* make the perfect end to a tapas party and armed with a piping bag and thermometer you will get light, crispy doughnuts. Do try them as they are great fun to make. Did you know it is mandatory to include brownies at a picnic? My *Chocolate Brownies* are quick to prepare. I could talk all day about this chapter, but instead I will leave you to cook.

Whether you are sharing with one other or a crowd, I do hope you find something to please. Have fun cooking, eating and sharing these recipes.

Best wishes,

Julia

PS Share your Vegan Tapas creations online using #VeganTapas.

Cook's notes

The following notes may assist you in your cooking. If you are vegan you will know to look for vegan versions of everything including ingredients such as chocolate, bread and wine, so I don't need to go into detail here. However, if you are uncertain or are cooking for a vegan, do feel free to contact me via http://veggietapas.com for further information or to help you source ingredients.

Bread crumbs To make fresh bread crumbs, remove the crusts from slices of bread. Place the bread in a food processor and process until you have crumbs. Use as per recipe. You can make your own dried bread crumbs by placing the processed crumbs on a baking tray. Place in a 150°C / 300°F / Gas Mark 2 oven for 20-30 minutes, until golden.

Canola oil A number of recipes use canola oil. If you cannot get hold of canola oil you can also use vegetable or sunflower oil. Please note canola oil and rapeseed oil are the same thing.

Cheese There are some fantastic brands of vegan cheese available which work really well in cooking. For these recipes I used Redwood's *Cheezly*, which melts really well and Vegusto's *No Moo* variety. I state the style of cheese suited for each recipe in the ingredients list, but don't be afraid to experiment.

Cream cheese Make sure your chosen brand of vegan cream cheese is suitable for baking with, if that is what the recipe calls for. I used *Tofutti Better Than Cream Cheese*, with great results.

Herbs Both fresh and dried herbs are used in the recipes. If you want to substitute one for the other, one 15ml tablespoon of fresh is equivalent to a 5ml teaspoon of dried. Try not to use dried parsley or basil; too much of the flavour is lost.

Margarine Use your preferred brand of vegan margarine or spread. Just make sure it is suitable for the purpose it is used for in the recipe. Not all spreads are suitable for frying or baking.

Milk Soy milk was used for those recipes containing milk. Do use your preferred dairy-free alternative, although results may vary.

Nutmeg Do use whole fresh nutmeg, never ground. The flavour is far superior. Use a fine grater to grate the nutmeg.

Pastry I use ready-made shortcrust and puff pastry for the recipes as well as sweet pastry cases. The pastry sheets are roughly 24cm (9½in) squares. To thaw the pastry, remove the amount of sheets you need from the freezer and stand for 10 minutes. Make sure when buying your pastry to check it is vegan. If you have a favourite pastry recipe, do feel free to use it, just remember you will need to blind bake the pastry before adding the filling.

To blind bake pastry cases, cut the pastry into 10cm (4in) rounds and press into the holes of a 12-hole muffin tin. Prick the pastry with a fork. Refrigerate for 30 minutes to help prevent shrinkage. Preheat the oven to 200°C / 400°F / Gas Mark 6. Place in the oven and cook the pastry for 10 minutes. Remove the tin from the oven and use the back of a teaspoon to press down on the pastry to remove any air pockets. Return to the oven and cook for another 10 minutes, until crisp and golden. Let the cases cool for a few minutes before transferring to a wire rack to cool completely.

Rather than weighing down the pastry with beans, I remove the pastry from the oven halfway through cooking and press any air out of the pastry. However, if you prefer you can weigh down the pastry. You will need to line each piece of pastry with baking paper then fill with dried rice or beans or ceramic baking beans used specifically for this purpose. Bake for 10 minutes, then remove the beans and baking paper and return to the oven for 10 minutes to crisp.

Pine nuts Some recipes call for toasted pine nuts. To do this, place your pine nuts in a frying pan. No need to add oil. Heat over a low heat until the nuts start to brown, shaking them occasionally. Do watch them as they will quickly go from brown to black if you are not careful.

Savoury yeast flakes These are available from health food stores. They are also known as nutritional yeast flakes.

Sterilising jars To sterilise jars, preheat the oven to 140°C / 275°F / Gas Mark 1. Wash the jars and lids in warm soapy water and rinse in warm water. Place the jars and lids facing downwards on the oven shelf. Leave them there for 10 minutes and then turn the oven off. The jars can stay in the oven until you are ready to use them. Remember to use oven gloves when handling the jars. Once cool, store your filled jars in the refrigerator.

Sugar If you live in the US you need to check your sugar is vegan. Sugar made in Australia and the UK is vegan.

Tofu Sometimes a recipe requires that the tofu is drained before using. To do this, remove the tofu from the pack and wrap in several sheets of paper towel. Place between two heavy chopping boards. You can add additional weight on top if you like. Let it drain for 30 minutes. Discard the paper towel and use as per the recipe.

Measures used

Recipes use cups, grams and millilitres.

The following conventions were used:

1 cup = 250ml

1 tablespoon = 15 ml

1 teaspoon = 5ml

Conversions

Grams to ounces	Millilitres to fluid ounces	Centimetres to inches
25g = 1 oz	60ml = 2 fl oz	1.5cm = ½in
50g = 1¾ oz	80ml = 2½ fl oz	2cm = ¾in
75g = 2¾ oz	100ml = 3½ fl oz	2.5cm = 1in
100g = 3½ oz	125ml = 4 fl oz	4cm = 1½in
125g = 4 oz	160ml = 5 fl oz	5cm = 2in
150g = 5 oz	180ml = 6 fl oz	6cm = 2½in
200g = 7 oz	200ml = 7 fl oz	8cm = 3in
250g = 8 oz	250ml = 8 fl oz	10cm = 4in
500g = 16 oz	500ml = 16 fl oz	20cm = 8in
1kg = 32 oz	1 litre = 32 fl oz	30cm = 12in

Oven temperatures for fan ovens

If you have a fan oven you can reduce temperatures by 10-20°C / 20-50°F. Consult your oven manual for precise instructions.

Don't get lost in translation

Wherever you are in the world, I hope you will be able to use my recipes. Below I have tried to list those ingredients whose names vary around the world.

Almond meal = ground almonds

Canola oil = rapeseed oil

Capsicum = bell pepper

Coriander = cilantro

Eggplant = aubergine

Plain flour = all-purpose flour

Self-raising flour = self-rising flour

Spring onions = green onions, salad onions, scallions, the long skinny one

Zucchini = courgette

DIPS

Recipes to accompany dips

Mayonnaise

Once you have made your own mayonnaise you will not look back. Just remember to soak some cashews overnight in the fridge.

½ cup / 75g raw cashews, soaked overnight in cold water
¼ cup / 60ml water
1 tablespoon lemon juice
1 teaspoon white wine vinegar
½ teaspoon Dijon mustard
Salt and freshly ground black pepper

1 Drain the soaked cashews and place in a food processor. Add the water, lemon juice, vinegar, mustard, a pinch of salt and a good grind of pepper. Blend thoroughly until the mixture is smooth. This will take a few minutes. Adjust the seasoning as needed. Transfer to a serving dish and refrigerate until needed.

~ Makes 1 cup ~

Chilli jam

This chilli jam is a hot one! If you are not keen on the heat you could always use a green chilli instead or chilli flakes, which means you can use as much or as little as you like. Goes well with puffed potato slices and crispy onion rings.

1 tablespoon olive oil
1 small onion, peeled and finely chopped
1 clove garlic, peeled and crushed
1 red chilli, seeded and finely chopped
2 tomatoes, seeded and finely chopped
1 tablespoon chopped fresh coriander
1 tablespoon balsamic vinegar
¼ cup / 50g brown sugar
Salt and freshly ground black pepper

1 Heat the olive oil in a small saucepan over a medium heat. Add the onion and garlic and cook until soft, about 10 minutes.

2 Add the chilli, tomatoes and coriander, stirring to combine. Stir in the vinegar and sugar. Bring to the boil, then reduce the heat and simmer for 20 minutes, until thickened, stirring occasionally. Season to taste with salt and freshly ground black pepper.

3 Leave to cool then serve. Once the chilli jam is cool, refrigerate until needed, but bring to room temperature before serving.

~ Makes 1 cup ~

Artichoke dip

This recipe is proof of how quickly a homemade dip can be made, minus all the unwanted ingredients often found in store-bought dips.

275g jar marinated artichoke hearts, drained
¼ cup / 60g silken tofu
1 clove garlic, peeled and crushed
2 tablespoons lemon juice
2 tablespoons pine nuts
1 teaspoon savoury yeast flakes
Freshly ground black pepper

1 In a food processor, blend together the artichoke hearts, tofu, garlic, lemon juice, pine nuts and savoury yeast flakes. Blend until smooth. Add pepper to taste. Serve.

~ **Makes 1 cup** ~

Tomato salsa

Once you realise how easy it is to make your own salsa, you will never buy store-bought again! The recipe requires you peel the tomatoes. I have found the easiest way to peel a tomato is with a vegetable peeler, provided the tomato is firm. Alternatively you can stand them in boiling water for a minute to loosen the skin, but I really do not think this is necessary.

4 tomatoes, peeled, seeded and finely chopped
1 green chilli, seeded and finely chopped
1 clove garlic, peeled and crushed
1 tablespoon chopped fresh coriander
Juice of 1 lime
1 tablespoon extra virgin olive oil
Salt and freshly ground black pepper

1 In a small bowl, mix together the tomatoes, green chilli, garlic, coriander, lime juice and olive oil. Mix well and season to taste with salt and freshly ground black pepper. Leave to stand for an hour to allow the flavours to develop. Serve.

~ Makes 1 cup ~

Minty cream dip

This dip is easy and full of flavour. Do not be afraid to use dried mint flakes, as the flavour still comes through. If you prefer to use fresh mint, use 3 tablespoons. Goes well with onion bhaji and falafel.

150g firm tofu
3 tablespoons soy milk
1 tablespoon lemon juice
1 tablespoon dried mint flakes
1 clove garlic, peeled and crushed
1 tablespoon agave syrup
Pinch of chilli powder
Salt and freshly ground black pepper

1 In a blender or food processor, blend the tofu with the soy milk and lemon juice. Add the dried mint flakes, garlic, agave syrup and chilli powder. Blend until smooth. Season to taste. Serve.

~ Makes 1 cup ~

Blue 'cheese' dip

You can use your favourite brand of blue-style cheese for this recipe. Do use fresh chives if you have them.

---

1 cup / 100g grated vegan blue-style cheese
75g vegan cream cheese
2 tablespoons soy milk
1 teaspoon dried chives
Freshly ground black pepper

---

1 In a food processor blend together the blue-style cheese, cream cheese, milk and chives, until smooth and creamy. Season to taste with freshly ground black pepper. Serve.

~ Makes 1 cup ~

Aioli

Aioli is garlic mayonnaise and is just as easy to make as regular mayonnaise. It goes well with many recipes, although I particularly like it with bean and herb mini sausages and spiced potato wedges.

½ cup / 75g raw cashews, soaked overnight in cold water
¼ cup / 60ml water
3 cloves garlic, peeled and crushed
1 tablespoon lemon juice
1 teaspoon white wine vinegar
½ teaspoon Dijon mustard
Salt and freshly ground black pepper

1 Drain the soaked cashews and place in a food processor. Add the water, garlic, lemon juice, vinegar, mustard, a pinch of salt and a good grind of pepper. Blend thoroughly until the mixture is smooth. This will take a few minutes. Adjust the seasoning as needed. Transfer to a serving dish and refrigerate until needed.

~ Makes 1 cup ~

Cheesy dip

A combination of vegan cream cheese and vegan cheddar results in a tasty cheesy dip. Adding the tofu and milk ensures it makes a nice creamy texture.

125g vegan cream cheese
½ cup / 50g grated vegan cheddar-style cheese
60g firm tofu
3 tablespoons soy milk
1 teaspoon dried chives
½ teaspoon mustard powder
Freshly ground black pepper

1 Beat together the cream cheese and cheddar-style cheese in a small bowl. Place the tofu and milk in a food processor and process until smooth. Stir it into the cheese. Mix in the chives and mustard powder. Season liberally with freshly ground black pepper. Spoon into a serving bowl of your choice. Refrigerate until needed.

~ Makes 1 cup ~

Warm cheesy sauce

Inspired by the warm cheese you get with fondue, this sauce is also intended for dipping. No need to sit around a fondue pot however. You can give guests their own individual bowls of sauce for dipping, or allow guests to help themselves.

1 clove garlic, peeled
1 tablespoon corn flour
½ teaspoon mustard powder
2 tablespoons water
½ cup / 125ml vegan white wine
1½ cups / 150g vegan cheese, suitable for melting
Salt and freshly ground black pepper

1 Rub a small saucepan with a clove of garlic. Blend together the corn flour, mustard powder and water to form a paste. Add the paste to the saucepan with the white wine and bring to the boil, stirring with a wooden spoon.

2 Once the wine is boiling, reduce the heat, add the vegan cheese then simmer for 2 minutes, until the sauce is thick and creamy, stirring all the time. Season to taste. Serve.

~ Makes 1 cup ~

Beetroot dip

This colourful dip is full of flavour; the wasabi nicely complements the beetroot. You can add more if you wish, however take care as it can easily overpower the beetroot.

450g can sliced beetroot, drained
400g can butter beans, rinsed and drained
½ teaspoon wasabi paste
Salt and freshly ground black pepper

1 Tip the beetroot and butter beans into a food processor and add the wasabi. Process until the mixture is smooth. Season to taste with salt and black pepper. Spoon into a serving bowl. Refrigerate until needed.

~ Makes 2 cups ~

Lemony dip

This dip is slightly sweetened to offset the flavours of the tofu and lemon. You can add more or less sugar to taste. To keep the dip looking white, you may prefer to season with white rather than black pepper.

150g firm tofu
2 tablespoons soy milk
Finely grated peel and juice of 1 lemon
1 teaspoon caster sugar
Salt and freshly ground black pepper

1 Place the tofu and milk into a food processer and process until smooth. Add the lemon peel and juice and mix to combine. Stir in the sugar and season to taste. Serve.

~ Makes 1 cup ~

Guacamole

You can easily spice up this guacamole further by adding a teaspoon of chilli powder. Great as a dip, it also goes well as a topping for chickpea bites.

---

2 Hass avocados, halved and stones removed
1 small onion, peeled and cut into chunks
1 clove garlic, peeled and crushed
Juice of 1 lime
2 tablespoons fresh coriander
1 teaspoon ground cumin
1 tablespoon olive oil
1 teaspoon granulated sugar
Salt and freshly ground black pepper

---

1 Scoop the flesh of the avocados from the skin and place in a food processor. Add the onion and garlic and process until coarsely chopped. Add the lime juice, coriander, cumin, olive oil and sugar. Continue processing until the mixture is smooth and well combined. Season to taste with salt and freshly ground black pepper. Serve.

~ Makes 1 cup ~

Sweetcorn dip

Another quick to prepare dip, that uses canned corn kernels. Adding the spices means you lose the yellow colour, but this is made up for in the flavour.

310g can corn kernels, drained
2 tablespoons vegan cream cheese
1 clove garlic, peeled and crushed
¼ teaspoon chilli powder
¼ teaspoon smoked paprika
Freshly ground black pepper

1 In a food processor blend together the corn kernels, cream cheese, garlic, chilli powder and smoked paprika. Season to taste with freshly ground black pepper. Pour into a serving bowl of your choice. Refrigerate until needed.

~ Makes 1 cup ~

Spicy peanut dip

This peanut dip uses light coconut milk. Make sure to shake the can of coconut milk well before opening as you will not be using the full can. This dip goes well with crumbed tofu fingers.

½ cup / 150g crunchy peanut butter
1 clove garlic, peeled and crushed
1 teaspoon lemon juice
1 teaspoon ground cumin
½ teaspoon dried chilli flakes
½ teaspoon onion powder
⅓ cup / 80ml light coconut milk
Salt and freshly ground black pepper

1 In a bowl, mix together the peanut butter, garlic, lemon juice, cumin, dried chilli flakes and onion powder. Gradually add the coconut milk, stirring well to combine. Season to taste with salt and freshly ground black pepper. Serve.

~ Makes 1 cup ~

Hummus

Tahini (sesame paste) is traditionally used in hummus. For this recipe I have used unhulled tahini for a greater depth of flavour. Feel free to use regular tahini if you cannot get hold of the unhulled variety.

400g can chickpeas, rinsed and drained
1 clove garlic, peeled and crushed
2 tablespoons unhulled tahini
2 tablespoons lemon juice
2 tablespoons extra virgin olive oil
¼ teaspoon smoked paprika
Salt and freshly ground black pepper

1 Place the chickpeas in a food processor and blend briefly to break them down. Add the garlic, tahini, lemon juice, olive oil and smoked paprika. Process well until smooth. If the hummus is quite thick add 1-2 tablespoons of water so it has a good dipping consistency. Season to taste with salt and freshly ground black pepper. Pour into a serving bowl and refrigerate until needed.

~ Makes just over 1 cup ~

Tomato and onion relish

Grab an onion and store cupboard ingredients and you have yourself a tasty relish. If you are not intending to use all the relish at once, you can pour the relish into a sterilised jar and store it in the fridge until needed.

1 tablespoon olive oil
1 onion, peeled and chopped
400g can chopped tomatoes
½ teaspoon smoked paprika
1 tablespoon red wine vinegar
1 tablespoon brown sugar
Salt and freshly ground black pepper

1 Heat the olive oil in a saucepan over a medium heat. Add the onion and fry for 4 minutes, until pale and soft.

2 Stir in the chopped tomatoes, smoked paprika, red wine vinegar and brown sugar. Bring to the boil. Reduce the heat and let the mixture simmer for 30 minutes, until thick and glossy. Season to taste with salt and freshly ground black pepper. Transfer to a serving bowl or sterilised jar and leave to cool. Serve.

~ Makes 1 cup ~

Tzatziki

Tzatziki is a refreshing cucumber-based dip. I have used Lebanese cucumber for this recipe. If you cannot find it feel free to use a regular cucumber. Tzatziki goes well with falafel, baked samosa and onion bhaji.

2 Lebanese cucumbers, about 250g
150g firm tofu
½ tablespoon white wine vinegar
1 tablespoon chopped fresh mint
1 tablespoon lemon juice
1 tablespoon extra virgin olive oil
1 clove garlic, peeled and crushed
Salt and freshly ground black pepper

1 Peel the cucumber, cut into chunks and add to a food processor. Process briefly until the cucumber is coarsely chopped. Place in a bowl.

2 Place the tofu and vinegar in the food processor and process until smooth. Stir the tofu into the cucumber. Add the mint, lemon juice, olive oil and garlic. Stir well to combine and season to taste with salt and freshly ground black pepper. Refrigerate until needed.

~ Makes 1 cup ~

Sweet chilli sauce

Realising how many recipes would go well with sweet chilli sauce, I thought you might like to make your own. This recipe is sweet with a kick of heat, unlike the sickly sauces you often find in bottles.

100g red chillies, stalks removed, seeded and roughly chopped
340g jar mixed pickled chillies, drained
2 cloves garlic, peeled
1 cup / 250ml white vinegar
1 cup / 200g granulated sugar
¼ cup / 60ml water, plus ⅓ cup / 80ml for thinning sauce
1 teaspoon salt

1 In a food processor, add the red chillies, mixed pickled chillies and garlic. Process until the chillies and garlic are finely chopped. Add to a medium sized saucepan, together with the vinegar, sugar, water and salt.

2 Bring to the boil, then reduce the heat to medium-low and simmer for 40 minutes, until thickened. Remove from the heat and cool for 5 minutes. Use a stick blender to blend the mixture until it is smooth. Stir in ⅓ cup / 80ml of water to give it a saucy consistency.

3 Pour the sauce into a sterilised jar and leave to cool. When cool, spoon as much as you need into your choice of serving dish.

~ Makes 1½ cups ~

TOPPINGS

Recipes for topping

Roasted tomatoes and olives

Roasting the tomatoes and olives gives them a lovely depth of flavour. You will expect the tomatoes to collapse as this makes them easier to use as a topping. They make a great topping for bruschetta and polenta.

250g cherry tomatoes, cut into halves
2 tablespoons olive oil
1 clove garlic, peeled and crushed
Salt and freshly ground black pepper
½ cup / 80g pitted black olives, sliced
1 tablespoon chopped fresh basil

Preheat the oven to 200°C / 400°F / Gas Mark 6

1 Place the tomatoes in a small roasting pan. Combine the olive oil and garlic and pour it over the tomatoes, ensuring they are coated with the oil. Season with salt and pepper. Roast in the oven for 25 minutes.

2 Remove from the oven, and stir in the olives and basil. Roast for another 15 minutes. Serve warm.

~ **Makes 1 cup (enough for 8 bruschetta)** ~

Mushroom pâté

The cashews and red wine give an extra depth to this pâté. I use Swiss browns as I prefer their flavour to regular white mushrooms. Feel free to use your favourite mushroom variety in this recipe.

1 tablespoon olive oil
1 onion, peeled and chopped
1 clove garlic, peeled and crushed
150g Swiss brown mushrooms, sliced
1 tablespoon vegan red wine
2 tablespoons raw cashews
1 teaspoon chopped fresh parsley
Salt and freshly ground black pepper
2 tablespoons vegan cream cheese

1 Heat the olive oil in a frying pan over a medium heat. Add the onion and garlic and cook for 5 minutes, until pale and soft. Add the mushrooms and continue cooking for 3-4 minutes, until the mushrooms are soft. Stir in the red wine, letting it cook for 1 minute. Remove from the heat and leave to cool for about 10 minutes.

2 Tip the mushrooms into a food processor, together with the cashews, parsley and seasoning. Blend until the ingredients come together in a smooth consistency. Add the cream cheese and blend until combined. Spoon into a serving bowl and refrigerate until needed.

~ Makes 1 cup ~

Pea pâté

Although a pea pâté sounds uninteresting and simplistic, I encourage you to try it. I think you will be pleasantly surprised.

1 cup / 125g frozen peas
1 tablespoon chopped fresh mint
Whole nutmeg
75g vegan cream cheese
Salt and freshly ground black pepper

1 Bring a saucepan of water to the boil. Add the peas and cook for 3 minutes. Drain then leave to cool.

2 Tip the peas into a food processor with the mint and a good grating of nutmeg. Blend until the peas are nicely mashed. Add the cream cheese and process until the mixture is well combined and smooth. Season to taste. Serve. You can store the pâté in the refrigerator until needed.

~ Makes 1 cup ~

'Cheese' with tomatoes and basil

This quick to prepare topping goes lovely with bruschetta or polenta. As there is no cooking, it is merely a case of assembling the ingredients. If you can, use vine-ripened tomatoes for maximum flavour.

2 tomatoes, sliced
12 basil leaves
100g vegan mozzarella-style cheese, sliced
Extra virgin olive oil
Freshly ground black pepper

1 Divide the tomato slices between 6 pieces of your choice of bread or polenta. Top with the basil leaves, then finally the mozzarella-style cheese. Drizzle with olive oil and finish with a good grind of black pepper. Serve.

~ **Makes 6** ~

Bean pâté

This bean pâté is easy to prepare, but full of flavour. You could experiment with different beans if you like. Borlotti beans would work well.

400g can kidney beans, rinsed and drained
3 spring onions, chopped
1 clove garlic, peeled and crushed
2 tablespoons tomato paste
2 teaspoons lime juice
1 teaspoon smoked paprika
½ teaspoon chilli powder
Salt and freshly ground black pepper

1 Place the kidney beans and spring onions into a food processor. Process until they are roughly chopped. Add the garlic, tomato paste, lime juice, smoked paprika and chilli powder. Process until smooth. Season to taste with salt and freshly ground black pepper. Serve.

~ Makes 1 cup ~

Blue 'cheese' pâté

A lovely rich pâté that will go well with galettes. Use your favourite vegan blue-style cheese for this recipe. You may like to bring the pâté up to room temperature before serving to maximise the flavours.

1 tablespoon vegan margarine
2 spring onions, chopped
¼ cup / 60ml vegan red wine
1 cup / 100g grated vegan blue-style cheese
1 teaspoon dried chives
1 teaspoon dried oregano
Freshly ground black pepper

1 Melt the margarine in a small saucepan. Add the spring onions and cook for 4 minutes, until soft. Add the red wine then simmer for 2 minutes. Remove from the heat then leave to cool for 2 minutes.

2 Tip the spring onions and wine into a food processor and add the blue-style cheese, chives, oregano and a good grind of black pepper. Process until smooth and well combined. Pour into ramekins or a serving bowl of your choice. Place in the refrigerator and chill until firm.

~ Makes 1 cup ~

'Cheese' and onion

Don't worry; this won't taste anything like a bag of cheese and onion chips. The flavours are far more subtle, but good nevertheless.

1 tablespoon olive oil
1 red onion, peeled and sliced
1 teaspoon dried thyme
150g vegan cheddar-style cheese, sliced
Freshly ground black pepper
Extra virgin olive oil, for drizzling

1 Heat the olive oil in a frying pan over a medium heat. Add the red onion and fry for 4 minutes, until pale and soft. Try not to let them brown. Stir in the thyme. Distribute the onions evenly over your chosen base.

2 Top with the cheddar-style cheese. Season with freshly ground black pepper and finish with a light drizzle of extra virgin olive oil. Serve.

~ Makes enough to top 6 bruschetta ~

Creamy pesto

Adding tofu to this pesto recipe gives it a lovely fresh taste, further enhanced by mint flakes. As well as using as a topping, you can also use this pesto as a dip.

---

1 bunch fresh basil leaves (about 1 cup)
2 cloves garlic, peeled
¼ cup / 35g pine nuts
1 tablespoon savoury yeast flakes
½ teaspoon dried mint flakes
1 teaspoon lemon juice
¼ cup / 60ml extra virgin olive oil
¼ cup / 60g firm tofu, crumbled
Salt and freshly ground black pepper

---

1 In a food processor, blend together the basil leaves, garlic, pine nuts, savoury yeast flakes, mint flakes and lemon juice. Gradually add the extra virgin olive oil, processing until the mixture is thick and well combined. Add the crumbled tofu and process briefly to make a nice creamy consistency. Season to taste with salt and freshly ground black pepper. Pour into a serving bowl. Refrigerate until needed. Serve.

~ Makes 1 cup ~

Avocado cream

Avocados with a hint of coconut. This is one to keep your guests guessing. Although a perfect topping for bruschetta and polenta wedges, you could also use this cream as a dip, if you wish.

2 Hass avocados
1 clove garlic, peeled and crushed
1 tablespoon lime juice
¼ cup / 60ml coconut cream
Salt and freshly ground black pepper

1 Cut each avocado in half. Remove the stone then scoop the flesh into a food processor. Add the garlic and lime juice and blend until smooth. Add the coconut cream and process again until the mixture is thick and creamy. Season to taste with salt and freshly ground black pepper. Pour into a serving bowl. Serve.

~ Makes 1 cup ~

Flavoured spreads

Parsley, sage, rosemary and thyme are used to make four different spreads. These spreads are perfect for bruschetta, crostini, Melba toast, pita bread and slices of baguette.

120g vegan margarine

1 tablespoon chopped fresh parsley
½ teaspoon lemon juice

1 tablespoon chopped fresh sage, or 1 teaspoon dried
¼ teaspoon onion powder

½ teaspoon dried rosemary
1 sun-dried tomato, finely chopped

1 tablespoon chopped fresh thyme, or 1 teaspoon dried
½ teaspoon lemon juice

1 Beat the margarine with a wooden spoon until it is fluffy. Then divide the mixture into 4 equal portions.

2 To the first portion of margarine, mix in the parsley and lemon juice. Spoon into a serving dish and refrigerate until needed.

3 To the second portion, mix in the sage and onion powder. Spoon into a serving dish and refrigerate until needed.

4 To the third portion, mix in the rosemary and sun-dried tomato. Spoon into a serving dish and refrigerate until needed.

5 To the final portion, mix in the thyme and lemon juice. Spoon into a serving dish and refrigerate until needed.

~ Makes 1 cup in total ~

Kalamata tapenade

Big juicy kalamata olives go perfectly in this tapenade. If you cannot get hold of them, feel free to use your choice of black olives. Goes well with Melba toast and crostini.

1 cup / 160g pitted kalamata olives
¼ cup / 50g sun-dried tomatoes
1 teaspoon capers, rinsed and drained
1 clove garlic, peeled and crushed
1 tablespoon coarsely chopped fresh basil
1 tablespoon coarsely chopped fresh parsley
1 tablespoon lemon juice
1 tablespoon extra virgin olive oil
Freshly ground black pepper

1 Place the olives, sun-dried tomatoes, capers, garlic, basil, parsley, lemon juice and extra virgin olive oil into a food processor. Process until the mixture forms a paste. Season to taste with freshly ground black pepper. Spoon into a serving bowl. Serve.

~ Makes 1 cup ~

VEGETABLES

Crispy onion rings

You can prepare the onion rings in advance then reheat them on a baking tray in a 200°C / 400°F / Gas Mark 6 oven for 10 minutes.

2 large onions
½ cup / 125ml soy milk
½ cup / 75g polenta
½ teaspoon dried chilli flakes
1 teaspoon dried oregano
3 tablespoons canola oil

1 Peel and slice the onions into 1cm thick slices. Separate the rings.

2 Put the milk into a shallow bowl. Combine the polenta, chilli flakes and oregano on a plate. Dip the onion rings into the milk, then press into the polenta mixture, coating evenly.

3 Heat the canola oil in a large frying pan over a medium heat. Add the onions in batches and fry for 6 minutes, turning once. Drain on paper towel. Serve.

~ Makes about 30 ~

Garlic mushrooms

Garlic mushrooms are a classic tapas dish in Spain and are known as champinones al ajillo. The lemon juice in these mushrooms gives them an extra kick.

2 tablespoons olive oil
225g Swiss brown mushrooms, thickly sliced
3 cloves garlic, peeled and crushed
Finely grated peel and juice of ½ lemon
1 tablespoon chopped fresh parsley
Salt and freshly ground black pepper

1 Heat the olive oil in a large frying pan over a medium heat. Add the mushrooms and fry, stirring for 4 minutes, until they begin to soften.

2 Stir in the garlic, lemon peel, juice and parsley. Cook for 5 minutes, until the mushrooms are soft and cooked. Season to taste. Serve in a large bowl for sharing or use as a topping on polenta or bruschetta.

~ Makes 1 cup ~

Marinated capsicum strips

For this recipe, you will need to remove the skin from the capsicums. I show you an easy way of doing this that does not require trying to grill a whole capsicum then steaming in a bag afterwards.

1 red capsicum
1 yellow capsicum

For the marinade:
1 tablespoon balsamic vinegar
1 tablespoon extra virgin olive oil
1 clove garlic, peeled and crushed
1 teaspoon capers, rinsed and drained
1 tablespoon chopped fresh parsley
Freshly ground black pepper

Preheat the grill

1 Cut each capsicum into 4. Remove the stalk, seeds and membrane. Flatten each piece, to aid even grilling. Place on a wire grill tray, skin side up and grill for about 10 minutes, until the skin is blackened and blistered.

2 Once the capsicums are cool enough to handle, remove the skin, using a knife to help you. Slice the capsicum into bite-size strips, then place in a bowl.

3 To make the marinade, in a small bowl or jar, mix together the balsamic vinegar, olive oil, garlic, capers, parsley and a good grind of black pepper. Pour the marinade over the capsicum strips, making sure the strips are thoroughly coated with the mixture. Cover with plastic wrap and leave to stand for an hour to let the flavours come together. Serve.

~ Makes 2 cups ~

Polenta fried tomatoes

Make sure you use firm tomatoes to ensure they do not fall apart when frying. Just so you know, the polenta mix will not coat the skin of the tomatoes.

4 large tomatoes
½ cup / 75g polenta
1 teaspoon dried oregano
½ teaspoon garlic powder
Freshly ground black pepper
2 tablespoons olive oil

1 Thickly slice the tomatoes, about 1.5cm thick.

2 In a bowl, combine the polenta, oregano, garlic powder and a good grind of black pepper. Press the tomatoes into the polenta mixture to coat.

3 Heat the olive oil in a large frying pan over a medium heat. Add the tomatoes and fry for 2-3 minutes on each side until golden. Serve warm.

~ **Makes 20** ~

Roasted olives

I use a combination of green and kalamata olives for this recipe. You can use any combination of olives. Don't forget to put out a bowl for the stones if your olives are not pitted.

1 tablespoon olive oil
1 tablespoon balsamic vinegar
1 clove garlic, peeled and crushed
1 teaspoon dried rosemary
1 teaspoon dried chilli flakes
1 teaspoon capers, drained
Juice of 1 lemon
½ cup / 80g green olives stuffed with pimento
½ cup / 80g kalamata olives

Preheat the oven to 200°C / 400°F / Gas Mark 6

1 In a jar or small bowl, mix together the olive oil, vinegar, garlic, rosemary, chilli flakes, capers and lemon juice.

2 Place the olives on a roasting tray and add the prepared flavourings. Roast in the oven for about 20 minutes, until the olives begin to wrinkle. Spoon into a serving bowl and serve warm or cold with cocktail sticks.

~ Makes 1 cup ~

Stuffed jalapeños

Not for the faint-hearted, these peppers pack a punch. I have double-crumbed them to give a nice crunchy coating.

12 whole jalapeño peppers
200g vegan cream cheese
1 clove garlic, peeled and crushed
¼ cup / 35g dried bread crumbs
¼ cup / 40g polenta
2 tablespoons savoury yeast flakes
½ teaspoon smoked paprika
¼ cup / 40g plain flour
½ cup / 125ml soy milk
1 cup / 250ml canola oil

1 Make a slice down one side of each pepper. Remove as much of the seeds and membrane as you can. Keep the stalk intact.

2 In a small bowl, mix together the cream cheese and garlic. Use a teaspoon to fill the peppers. Do not overfill; you want to make sure they can close again.

3 On a plate, mix together the bread crumbs, polenta, savoury yeast flakes and smoked paprika. Place the flour on another plate and the milk in a separate bowl. One at a time, dip the peppers in the flour, then the milk then roll in the bread crumb mixture. Then dip into the flour again, then the milk and once more cover in bread crumbs.

4 Heat the oil in a large deep-sided frying pan over a medium heat. Add the peppers then fry until golden, turning as needed. This will take about 4-5 minutes. Drain on paper towel. Serve.

~ Makes 12 ~

Tomato and onion stuffed mushrooms

For this recipe I use mushrooms that are about 8cm in diameter. As such, you get bite-size mushrooms but still room enough for the stuffing. You can use whatever size mushrooms you prefer.

8 Swiss brown mushrooms, about 250g
2 tablespoons olive oil
1 red onion, peeled and chopped
1 clove garlic, peeled and crushed
1 tomato, seeded and chopped
1 cup / 60g fresh bread crumbs
1 teaspoon dried mixed herbs
Salt and freshly ground black pepper
Extra virgin olive oil, for drizzling

Preheat the grill

1 Remove the stalks from the mushrooms. You will use the stalks for the stuffing so coarsely chop, then set them aside. Heat 1 tablespoon of the olive oil in a large frying pan over a medium heat. Season the mushrooms then fry for 1 minute on each side until slightly softened. Remove from the pan then drain on paper towel.

2 Heat the rest of the olive oil, add the red onion and garlic and fry for 5 minutes, until soft. Add the mushroom stalks and cook for another 2 minutes. Tip into a bowl.

3 To the onions, add the tomatoes, bread crumbs, mixed herbs, a pinch of salt and a good grind of black pepper. Mix well to combine. Spoon the stuffing over the mushrooms and place on a wire grill tray. Drizzle with extra virgin olive oil and grill for 2-3 minutes, until golden. Serve warm.

~ Makes 8 ~

Squashed squash

Butternut squash is roasted then formed into bite-size fritters. Roasting the squash gives it extra flavour, so is worth doing. Since there is no peeling or chopping required, you can quickly get the squash in the oven, allowing you to get on with other tasks.

½ butternut squash, about 1kg
Olive oil, for drizzling
1 teaspoon allspice
Whole nutmeg
Salt and freshly ground black pepper
¼ cup / 40g corn flour
3 tablespoons canola oil

Preheat the oven to 200°C / 400°F / Gas Mark 6

1 Scoop the seeds from the squash. Place the squash on a roasting tray and drizzle with olive oil. Roast in the oven for about 1 hour, until tender. Test with a knife in the deepest section to ensure it is properly cooked.

2 Once the squash is cool enough to handle, use a large metal spoon to scoop the flesh into a bowl. Mash thoroughly using a potato masher, until all the lumps are removed. Mix in the allspice, a good grating of nutmeg, a pinch of salt and a good grind of black pepper. Stir in the corn flour.

3 Heat the canola oil in a large frying pan over a medium heat. Take tablespoons of the squash mixture and roll into balls. Flatten then add to the pan. Fry until golden and firm, about 3-4 minutes on each side. Drain on paper towel. Serve warm.

~ Makes 18 ~

Vegetable tempura

When making the tempura batter, make sure your water is ice cold. Remember to place a jug of water in the fridge beforehand, so you are well prepared. Feel free to vary the vegetables according to the season. You may also like to try: eggplant, asparagus, baby corn and pumpkin.

1 cup / 150g plain flour
Salt and freshly ground black pepper
1 cup / 250ml ice cold water
1 red capsicum, seeded and cut into large strips
½ cauliflower, cut into florets
1 head broccoli, cut into florets
1 onion, peeled and cut into 6 wedges
150g button mushrooms, wiped
Canola oil, for deep-frying

1 To make the batter, sift the flour into a bowl and stir in a pinch of salt and a good grind of black pepper. Add the water, then whisk to form a smooth batter.

2 Half-fill a wok with the canola oil and heat over a medium-high heat. Dip the vegetables into the batter then add to the wok. Take care to not overfill the wok. Fry until crispy. They will be quite pale. Remove with a slotted spoon and then drain on paper towel. Serve warm with a dip of your choice.

~ Makes plenty ~

Zucchini on sticks

The zucchini are sliced into strips and then threaded onto cocktail sticks. To give them extra flavour they are coated in smoked paprika and quickly griddled. Feel free to use your favourite spice for this recipe.

1 large zucchini
½ teaspoon smoked paprika
½ tablespoon olive oil

1 Cut the ends off the zucchini. Using a vegetable peeler, slice lengthwise down the zucchini to make long strips. You can discard the 1 or 2 strips that are mostly skin.

2 Thread the zucchini onto a cocktail stick, concertina style. Combine the smoked paprika and olive oil then brush it over the zucchini strips.

3 Heat a griddle pan until smoking. Add the zucchini and cook for 1-2 minutes on each side until slightly charred. Arrange on a serving plate and serve.

~ Makes about 14 ~

Crispy mushrooms

These mushrooms are flavoured with oregano and garlic powder and then shallow fried. Serve alone or with a dip of your choice (although mayonnaise is always good).

½ cup / 125 ml soy milk
¼ cup / 35g dried bread crumbs
1 teaspoon dried oregano
1 teaspoon garlic powder
Freshly ground black pepper
12 button mushrooms, about 100g
3 tablespoons canola oil

1 Place the milk in a bowl. On a plate, combine the bread crumbs, oregano and garlic powder. Add a good grind of black pepper.

2 Dip the mushrooms in the milk, coating completely, then cover in the bread crumbs.

3 Heat the canola oil in a large frying pan over a medium-high heat. Add the mushrooms and fry until they are crispy and golden, turning often. This will take about 5 minutes. Drain on paper towel. Serve.

~ Makes 12 ~

Roasted asparagus

Asparagus only takes a few minutes to roast and the flavour is far superior to what you get from boiling or steaming. If you like, you can barbecue the asparagus. You may like to serve these with a dip of your choice.

1 bunch asparagus, about 100g
1 tablespoon lemon juice
1 tablespoon olive oil
½ teaspoon ground ginger
Salt and freshly ground black pepper

Preheat the oven to 210°C / 410°F / Gas Mark 7

1 Snap off and discard the woody ends of the asparagus. Place the asparagus spears in a roasting tray.

2 In a small bowl or jar, mix together the lemon juice, olive oil and ground ginger. Season to taste with salt and freshly ground black pepper. Pour the mixture over the asparagus, coating evenly. Roast in the oven for 10 minutes, until they are just beginning to brown. Serve warm.

~ Makes about 12 ~

Grilled vegetable skewers

Since this is tapas, our skewers are cocktail sticks. Since you will only fit 2-3 veggies on each stick, a little will go a long way. I have provided you with a choice of vegetables and flavourings, but feel free to create your own.

Choice of vegetables:
Onion, thickly sliced
Red onion, thickly sliced
Capsicum (red, green or yellow), cut into 2cm sized pieces
Fennel, cut into 2cm sized pieces
Zucchini, sliced into 2cm chunks
Eggplant, sliced into 2cm chunks
Cherry tomatoes, kept whole or cut in half
Button mushrooms, cut in half
Pattypan squash, cut into quarters
Shallots, cut in half

Choice of flavourings:
1 tablespoon olive oil combined with either:

½ teaspoon garlic powder

½ teaspoon ground cumin and ½ teaspoon ground coriander

½ teaspoon ground turmeric and ½ teaspoon ground cumin

½ teaspoon smoked paprika

½ teaspoon salt and ½ teaspoon black pepper

Preheat the grill

1 Soak your cocktail sticks in water for 20 minutes to prevent them from burning. Thread 2 or 3 different vegetables onto each cocktail stick. Brush the vegetables with your choice of flavoured olive oil. Place on a wire grill tray.

2 Grill for 5-6 minutes, turning often, until the vegetables are tender and sizzling. Serve.

~ **Makes as many as you choose to prepare** ~

Eggplant bites

Confession time. I am not a fan of eggplant and I have tried it every which way. As such, this is the only dedicated eggplant recipe in the book. If you are not a fan of eggplant, give this recipe a go. Even I like it!

1 eggplant, about 250g
½ cup / 125ml soy milk
2 cups / 120g fresh bread crumbs
1 teaspoon sesame seeds
1 teaspoon dried oregano
1 teaspoon garlic powder
Freshly ground black pepper
3-6 tablespoons canola oil

1 Peel the eggplant and slice into 2cm rounds. Cut each round into halves or quarters, depending on their size.

2 Place the milk in a bowl. Place the bread crumbs on a plate and mix in the sesame seeds, oregano, garlic powder and a good grind of black pepper. Dip the eggplant into the milk and then roll in the bread crumbs.

3 Heat 3 tablespoons of the canola oil in a large frying pan over a medium heat. Add the eggplant and fry for 5 minutes, turning often, until golden brown all over. You may need to add more oil when cooking the second batch of eggplant as eggplants are the sponges of the veggie world. Drain on paper towel. Serve.

~ **Makes about 30 pieces** ~

Marinated olives

Cheer up olives with your own marinade. You will need to prepare the olives in advance to give them a few days to absorb the flavours. Use a sterilised jar and they will keep well until you need them. The olive oil will solidify in the fridge, but all will be well when it is brought up to room temperature. No need to chop the herbs for this recipe.

1 cup / 160g pitted black olives, rinsed and drained
2 tablespoons fresh lemon thyme
2 tablespoons fresh oregano
1 teaspoon grated lemon peel
1 clove garlic, peeled and crushed
1 teaspoon dried chilli flakes
Extra virgin olive oil

1 In a sterilised jar big enough to hold the olives, place half of the lemon thyme and oregano. Add the lemon peel, garlic and chilli flakes, followed by the black olives. Top with the rest of the herbs. Pour enough extra virgin oil into the jar to cover the olives. Put the lid on and give the jar a gentle shake to help mix the flavours. Place in the refrigerator for at least a day.

2 When you are ready to serve the olives, bring the jar to room temperature. Drain the olives from the oil, discarding the herbs. Place in a serving bowl and serve.

~ Makes 1 cup ~

Crudités

Crudités are a selection of raw vegetables, perfect for dipping. I have listed below a variety of vegetables that would work well. Choose your preferences, remembering that veg in season will be tastier and cheaper.

Cherry tomatoes, kept whole
Button mushrooms, kept whole
Baby carrots, kept whole
Celery stalks, sliced into sticks
Carrots, peeled and sliced into sticks
Cucumber, sliced into sticks
Red, green or yellow capsicum, seeded and sliced into strips
Asparagus, woody ends snapped off
Broccoli, cut into small florets
Cauliflower, cut into small florets
Radishes, root and leaf removed
Spring onions, root and floppy green leaves removed

1 Wash all vegetables. If you are using button mushrooms, wipe them down with damp paper towel. Prepare as directed above. You may like to store chopped vegetables in a bowl of water in the refrigerator if you are not using them immediately. This will keep them crisp. Arrange on a serving platter with your choice of dips.

~ Makes as much or as little as you choose ~

Crispy mixed herbs

You will want to use large leaves for this recipe, so you may need to use what is in season. Make sure your herbs are thoroughly dry before frying, to cut down on spitting oil. Serve with spicy roasted nuts for a contrast.

½ cup / small bunch fresh sage leaves
½ cup / small bunch fresh basil leaves
½ cup / small bunch fresh parsley leaves
½ cup / small bunch fresh mint leaves
3 tablespoons canola oil
½ teaspoon sea salt flakes

---

1 Remove all herbs from their stalks, making sure they are clean and dry.

2 Heat the canola oil in a large frying pan over a medium-high heat. Using tongs, add the herbs in batches and fry for 1 minute. Try not to let them go brown. Drain on paper towel. Transfer to a serving dish and sprinkle with sea salt flakes. Serve.

~ Makes 1 cup ~

TOFU

AND

'CHEESE'

Classic tortilla

I call this a classic tortilla simply because of the flavours used – onion and potato. Clearly there is nothing classic about using tofu, but it tastes good regardless!

450g potatoes
1 tablespoon olive oil
1 large onion, peeled and sliced
450g firm tofu, crumbled
½ cup / 125ml soy milk
1 tablespoon corn flour
½ teaspoon smoked paprika
Salt and freshly ground black pepper

Preheat the oven to 180°C / 350°F / Gas Mark 4

1 Bring a large saucepan of lightly salted water to the boil. Peel then thinly slice the potatoes. Cut each slice in half. Add the potatoes to the saucepan and once the water comes back up to the boil, parboil for 5 minutes. Drain.

2 Heat the olive oil in a deep-sided frying pan over a medium heat. Fry the onion for 3-4 minutes, until pale. Add the potatoes and stir to coat them in the oil. Turn the heat down to low. Put the lid on and continue cooking until the potatoes are tender, about 7-8 minutes. Stir occasionally.

3 Place the tofu, milk, corn flour and paprika in a food processor. Process until smooth. Stir the mixture into the onions and potatoes and season. Tip the mixture into a greased and lined 15 x 20cm deep-sided dish. Bake for 35 minutes, until golden and firm.

4 Leave to cool in the pan before removing then slicing into16 pieces. Serve.

~ **Makes 16** ~

Tofu cubes with agave syrup

The agave syrup offsets the taste and texture of the tofu making this quick to prepare dish very moreish.

100g firm tofu, drained
Salt and freshly ground black pepper
¼ cup / 35g roasted unsalted cashews
Agave syrup, to serve

1 Slice the tofu into 8 even-sized pieces. Season with salt and black pepper.

2 Place the cashews into a food processor and process until coarsely ground.

3 Place the cashews on a plate and coat each tofu cube with the cashews.

4 Put on a serving plate. Just before serving, drizzle with agave syrup.

~ Makes 8 ~

Mushroom and red onion tortilla

The addition of sun-dried tomatoes in this recipe gives extra flavour and texture. Because of their strong flavours you do not need to add many to make an impact.

1 tablespoon olive oil
1 red onion, peeled and sliced
1 clove garlic, peeled and crushed
150g mushrooms, sliced
¼ cup / 50g sun-dried tomatoes, chopped
1 tablespoon chopped fresh parsley
450g firm tofu, crumbled
½ cup / 125ml soy milk
1 tablespoon corn flour
Salt and freshly ground black pepper

Preheat the oven to 180°C / 350°F / Gas Mark 4

1 Heat the olive oil in a large frying pan over a medium heat. Add the onion and garlic and fry for 5 minutes, until soft. Add the mushrooms and cook until the mushrooms are golden, about 4-5 minutes. Stir in the sun-dried tomatoes and parsley and cook for another minute.

2 Place the tofu, milk and corn flour in a food processor. Process until smooth. Stir the mixture into the onions and mushrooms and season well. Tip the mixture into a greased and lined 15 x 20cm deep-sided dish. Bake for 35 minutes, until golden and firm.

3 Leave to cool in the pan before slicing into 16 pieces. Serve.

~ Makes 16 ~

Marinated tofu sticks

Serve these tofu sticks with a dip of your choice, although lemony dip or tomato salsa will both work particularly well.

350g firm tofu, drained

For the marinade:
1 clove garlic, peeled and crushed
1 teaspoon dried thyme
1 teaspoon dried rosemary
1 teaspoon onion powder
2 tablespoons olive oil
1 teaspoon lemon juice
Freshly ground black pepper

2 tablespoons canola oil
2 teaspoons sesame seeds

1 Slice the tofu into 2cm wide strips and then cut each strip in half lengthwise to make 10 strips in total. Arrange on a plate.

2 In a jar or small bowl mix together the garlic, thyme, rosemary, onion powder, olive oil, lemon juice and a good grind of black pepper. Pour the marinade over the tofu, turning the pieces to coat them in the flavours. Cover with plastic wrap and refrigerate for an hour, giving the tofu time to absorb the flavours.

3 Heat the canola oil in a large frying pan over a medium heat. Sprinkle the sesame seeds over the tofu sticks then add to the pan. Cook until golden brown on each side, about 8 minutes in total. Remove from the pan then cut in half to make bite-size sticks. Serve.

~ Makes 20 ~

Capsicum and tomato tortilla

A juicy red capsicum, tomato and onion can be found in this tortilla. To make it even more colourful, you could add some green and yellow capsicum.

1 tablespoon olive oil
1 onion, peeled and sliced
1 clove garlic, peeled and crushed
1 red capsicum, seeded and chopped
1 large tomato, chopped
450g firm tofu, crumbled
½ cup / 125ml soy milk
1 tablespoon corn flour
1 teaspoon dried oregano
Salt and freshly ground black pepper

Preheat the oven to 180°C / 350°F / Gas Mark 4

1 Heat the olive oil in a large frying pan over a medium heat. Add the onion and fry for 4 minutes, until soft. Add the garlic and capsicum and fry until the capsicum starts to soften, about 5 minutes. Stir in the tomato.

2 Place the tofu, milk, corn flour and oregano in a food processor. Process until smooth. Stir the mixture into the onions, capsicum and tomato and season well. Tip the mixture into a greased and lined 15 x 20cm deep-sided dish. Bake for 35 minutes, until golden and firm.

3 Leave to cool in the pan before slicing into 16 pieces. Serve.

~ Makes 16 ~

Marinated tofu, avocado and tomato skewers

This is one of those simple snacks that is unexpectedly flavourful. If you like, you can drizzle any remaining marinade over the prepared skewers.

For the marinade:
2 tablespoons extra virgin olive oil
1 tablespoon lemon juice
1 clove garlic, peeled and crushed
1 teaspoon dried oregano
1 teaspoon sugar
Freshly ground black pepper

180g firm tofu, drained
1 Hass avocado
2 tablespoons lemon juice
16 cherry tomatoes (about 120g)

1 In a bowl, mix together the olive oil, lemon juice, garlic, oregano, sugar and a good grind of black pepper. Slice the tofu into 16 cubes and add them to the marinade. Make sure the tofu is coated evenly. Refrigerate for an hour.

2 Halve the avocado and remove the stone. Using a melon baller, scoop out 16 rounds from the avocado. Alternatively, dice into 2cm pieces. Pour the lemon juice over the avocado to help prevent the avocado from browning.

3 On each cocktail stick, thread a cube of tofu, avocado piece and cherry tomato. You may need to halve the cherry tomatoes if they are quite large. Arrange on a serving plate and serve.

~ Makes 16 ~

Cold rolls

The vegetables used in this recipe are not cooked, making the cold rolls refreshing and light. They are great to serve early on in your meal. Goes well with sweet chilli sauce or chilli jam.

1 small carrot
75g firm tofu, drained
3 spring onions
2 tablespoons bean sprouts
Salt and freshly ground black pepper
8 rice paper rounds

1 Peel the carrot and slice thinly into matchstick-sized pieces about 2cm long. Slice the tofu into similar sized pieces. Finely slice the spring onions. Place in a small bowl with the bean sprouts and stir together being careful not to break up the tofu. Season with salt and a good grind of black pepper.

2 Fill a shallow dish with lukewarm water for soaking the rice paper. Taking one round at a time, place in the water and soak for 30 seconds until soft. Have ready a tea towel to lay the rice paper on to drain. You want them flat and not folded, so take care here as they do get sticky.

3 Whilst on the tea towel, take a heaped tablespoon of the mixture and place at the bottom of the rice paper leaving a 1cm gap at the bottom and sides. Fold the bottom piece over the mixture then fold in the sides. From here roll the whole thing up to form your cold roll. Continue with the other ingredients, soaking each rice paper first. To speed the process up you can soak a paper whilst filling another. Serve.

~ Makes 8 ~

Devilled tofu

These pieces of tofu are very moreish; they may even convert non-tofu fans. Cooking the strips before cutting them makes frying the tofu more manageable.

For the marinade:
1 teaspoon Dijon mustard
2 tablespoons tomato ketchup
1 tablespoon soy sauce
½ tablespoon agave syrup
1 clove garlic, peeled and crushed
Pinch of chilli powder

350g firm tofu, drained
2 tablespoons olive oil

1 In a bowl or jar mix together the Dijon mustard, tomato ketchup, soy sauce, agave syrup, garlic and a pinch of chilli powder.

2 Slice the tofu into 2cm strips. Place on a plate and pour the marinade over the strips, making sure both sides are covered. Cover with plastic wrap and leave to marinate in the refrigerator for an hour.

3 Heat the olive oil in a large frying pan over a medium-high heat. Add the tofu, cooking for about 5 minutes on each side until crispy.

4 Remove the tofu from the pan and slice each strip into 4 bite-size pieces. These can then be put on cocktail sticks. Serve.

~ Makes 20 ~

Oven-baked savoury tofu bites

You will need to get hold of liquid smoke for this recipe, but it will be worth it. In Australia, you can find it in specialty food stores; else you may need to go online. Savoury yeast flakes are found in health food stores.

350g firm tofu, drained
2 tablespoons soy sauce
1 teaspoon liquid smoke
¼ cup / 40g plain flour
¼ cup / 10g savoury yeast flakes
1 teaspoon onion powder
1 teaspoon garlic powder
Freshly ground black pepper
Olive oil spray

1 Cut the tofu into 2cm slices. Cut each slice into 4 to make bite-size pieces. Arrange on a plate.

2 In a jar or small bowl mix the soy sauce with the liquid smoke. Pour the mixture over the tofu, making sure the pieces are evenly coated. Place in the refrigerator and let the tofu marinate for 30 minutes, or longer if you prefer.

Preheat the oven to 180°C / 350°F / Gas Mark 4

3 In a bowl, combine the flour, savoury yeast flakes, onion powder, garlic powder and a good grind of black pepper. Dip each pieces of tofu into the flour mix, then place on a baking tray lined with baking paper. Spray the tofu with olive oil.

4 Bake in the oven for 30 minutes. Remove and turn the pieces. Spray with some more olive oil and bake for a further 20 minutes, until firm.

5 Remove from the oven and add a cocktail stick to each piece and arrange on a serving plate. Serve.

~ **Makes 20** ~

Mini tofu burgers

These burgers are very simple to prepare. You could serve them as they are, with a topping of chilli jam or create your own burger buns. Use a cookie cutter to cut out rounds from a burger bun that match the size of your burgers.

300g firm tofu, drained
4 tablespoons olive oil
1 onion, peeled and chopped
1 clove garlic, peeled and crushed
¼ cup / 40g plain flour
1 teaspoon soy sauce
1 teaspoon chilli powder
Freshly ground black pepper

1 Crumble the tofu into a medium bowl.

2 Heat 1 tablespoon of the olive oil in a large frying pan over a medium heat. Add the onion and garlic and fry for about 7 minutes, until softened and brown. Add to the tofu.

3 To the tofu and onions, mix in the flour, soy sauce, chilli powder and a good grind of black pepper. Take a heaped tablespoon of the mixture and form it into a ball, then press down slightly to make a burger shape. Repeat with the rest of the mixture.

4 Heat the rest of the olive oil in the frying pan over a medium heat. Add the burgers and cook, turning once until they are brown. This will take about 5 minutes. Drain on paper towel. Serve.

~ Makes 12 ~

Crumbed tofu fingers

These tofu fingers do not require marinating, so are quick to prepare. I use regular firm tofu for this recipe; however you could use one of the flavoured tofu packs that are available. You can also add herbs and spices to the bread crumbs.

350g firm tofu, drained
3 tablespoons plain flour
Salt and freshly ground black pepper
½ cup / 125ml soy milk
1 cup / 60g fresh bread crumbs
3 tablespoons canola oil

1 Slice the tofu into 2cm wide strips and then cut each strip in half lengthwise to make 10 strips in total.

2 Place the flour on a plate and season with salt and a grind of black pepper. Place the milk in a bowl and the bread crumbs on another plate. Evenly coat the tofu with the flour, dip into the milk and then coat in the bread crumbs, shaking off any excess.

3 Heat the canola oil in a large frying pan over a medium heat. Add the tofu strips and then fry on all sides until the tofu is golden. This will take about 8 minutes in total. Drain on paper towel. Serve.

~ **Makes 10** ~

Sweet-and-sour tofu bites

This is tofu and pineapple on sticks; a flavoursome variation of the classic cheese and pineapple. The sweet-and-sour marinade on the tofu perfectly complements the pineapple.

225g can pineapple pieces in juice
2 tablespoons tomato paste
1 tablespoon white wine vinegar
2 teaspoons granulated sugar
2 teaspoons soy sauce
350g firm tofu, drained
2 tablespoons olive oil

1 Drain the pineapple juice into a bowl. Set aside the pineapple pieces.

2 To the pineapple juice, add the tomato paste, white wine vinegar, sugar and soy sauce. Mix well.

3 Cut the tofu into 2cm thick slices. Place on a bowl or plate. Pour the marinade over the tofu, making sure the tofu is covered on both sides. Cover with plastic wrap and refrigerate for an hour.

4 Heat the olive oil in a large frying pan over a medium-high heat. Add the tofu strips and fry until golden on both sides, about 10 minutes in total.

5 Remove the tofu from the pan and cut each slice into 4 to make bite-size pieces.

6 Take a piece of pineapple and skewer it on to a cocktail stick, then add a piece of tofu. Arrange on a plate and then serve.

~ Makes 20 ~

Citrus and herb tofu bites

Give tofu some zing with this zesty marinade. When frying the tofu, feel free to pour over the remaining marinade to make the most of the herbs you have used. Just take care as the oil will spit.

350g firm tofu, drained

For the marinade:
Grated peel and juice of 1 lemon
1 tablespoon lime juice
1 clove garlic, peeled and crushed
2 tablespoons olive oil
1 tablespoon chopped fresh parsley
1 tablespoon chopped fresh thyme
Salt and freshly ground black pepper

2 tablespoons olive oil, for frying

1 Cut the tofu into 2cm thick slices. Place on a plate.

2 In a small bowl, whisk together the lemon peel and juice, lime juice, garlic, olive oil, parsley and thyme. Season with salt and freshly ground black pepper. Pour the marinade over the tofu pieces, making sure they are coated on both sides. Cover with plastic wrap and refrigerate for an hour.

3 Heat the olive oil in a large frying pan over a medium-high heat. Add the tofu and fry until golden on both sides, about 10 minutes in total. Remove the tofu from the pan and cut each slice into 4 to make bite-size pieces. If desired, pop them on cocktail sticks before arranging on a serving plate. Serve warm.

~ Makes 20 ~

Spicy tofu fingers

You will be amazed at how quickly these are eaten up. The flavours are sweet and spicy. If you want to serve them with a dip, try a refreshing tomato salsa.

350g firm tofu, drained

For the marinade:
2 tablespoons olive oil
2 tablespoons soy sauce
2 tablespoons sweet chilli sauce
1 tablespoon brown sugar
½ tablespoon grated fresh ginger
1 teaspoon ground cumin
1 teaspoon ground coriander
Freshly ground black pepper

2 tablespoons olive oil, for frying

1 Slice the tofu into 2cm wide strips and then cut each strip in half lengthwise to make 10 strips in total. Arrange on a plate.

2 Mix together the olive oil, soy sauce, sweet chilli sauce, brown sugar, ginger, cumin, coriander and a good grind of black pepper. Pour the mixture over the prepared tofu, turning to coat evenly. Cover with plastic wrap and leave to marinate in the refrigerator for an hour.

3 Heat the olive oil in a large frying pan over a medium-high heat. Using tongs as the oil will spit, add the tofu strips. Fry, turning once, until golden on both sides. This will take about 8 minutes in total. Serve.

~ **Makes 10** ~

Parmesan-style wafers

These flavourful wafers are simple to prepare. I suggest you use a cookie cutter to help you shape the wafers on the baking tray. If you like, you could try using different shapes for different effects.

1 cup / 100g grated vegan Parmesan-style cheese
1 teaspoon dried oregano
½ tablespoon plain flour
Freshly ground black pepper

Preheat the oven to 220°C / 425°F / Gas Mark 7

1 Mix together the Parmesan-style cheese, oregano and flour in a small bowl. Season with a good grind of black pepper.

2 Line 2 baking trays with baking paper. Using a 7cm round cookie cutter as a guide, sprinkle 2 teaspoonfuls of the mixture into the cutter to form a round. Repeat to form 24 rounds.

3 Bake for 7-8 minutes, until golden. Be careful not to burn them, so check frequently. Cool on the baking tray and then serve.

~ Makes 24 ~

Crumbed 'cheeses'

Coat vegan cheese in bread crumbs then deep-fry. The result are melted morsels of deliciousness encased in a crispy coating. Use your choice of vegan cheese and include a variety, if you wish. I used Cheezly which worked fantastically.

250g vegan cheese
¼ cup / 40g plain flour
Salt and freshly ground black pepper
½ cup / 125ml soy milk
½ cup / 70g dried bread crumbs
1 teaspoon dried oregano
1 cup / 250ml canola oil

1 Cut the vegan cheese into 2cm pieces.

2 Place the flour onto a plate and season well with salt and freshly ground black pepper. Place the milk into a bowl and the dried bread crumbs mixed with the oregano onto another plate. Coat each cheese evenly with the flour. Dip the floured cheeses into the milk then roll in the bread crumbs. Once again, coat in the flour, dip into the milk and then cover with bread crumbs.

3 Heat the canola oil in a large frying pan or wok, over a medium-high heat. Add the cheeses, a few at a time. Fry until golden brown, for about 3-4 minutes, turning frequently. Drain on paper towel, then serve warm.

~ Makes about 14 ~

GRAINS, PULSES AND NUTS

Vegetable paella

I had to include a paella recipe, even if it is not exactly bite-size. However it makes a great share dish, served on a platter from which guests can help themselves. I did consider calling this recipe 'Italian paella' given the wonderful red, white and green colours of this dish.

2 tablespoons olive oil
1 onion, peeled and chopped
1 clove garlic, peeled and crushed
1 red capsicum, seeded and chopped
1 green capsicum, seeded and chopped
150g button mushrooms, sliced
1 cup / 200g long grain rice
¼ cup / 35g pine nuts, toasted
⅓ cup / 55g green olives
2 tomatoes, seeded and chopped
2½ cups / 625ml vegetable stock
1 teaspoon smoked paprika
1 teaspoon dried oregano
Freshly ground black pepper

1 Heat the olive oil in a large deep-sided frying pan over a medium heat. Add the onion and garlic and fry for 4 minutes, until pale and soft.

2 Add the capsicums and mushrooms and cook for a further 4 minutes.

3 Add the rice, stirring into the vegetables and cook for 2 minutes.

4 Add the pine nuts, olives, tomatoes, stock, paprika and oregano. Season with freshly ground black pepper. Bring to the boil. Turn the heat down slightly and simmer for 15 minutes, stirring occasionally until the rice is cooked and all the stock is absorbed. Let cool slightly before serving.

~ Makes over 2 cups ~

Capsicums stuffed with pearl couscous

Unlike regular couscous, you cook pearl couscous the same way you would pasta, adding it to a pan of boiling water. If you cannot find pearl couscous, you can use couscous in this recipe instead.

3 red capsicums
2 tablespoons olive oil, plus extra for drizzling
1 onion, peeled and chopped
¾ cup / 100g pearl couscous
125g can corn kernels, rinsed and drained
1 avocado, skin and stone removed, chopped
1 tomato, chopped
1 tablespoon pine nuts, toasted
1 teaspoon dried mint flakes
½ tablespoon lemon juice
Salt and freshly ground black pepper

Preheat the oven to 210°C / 410°F / Gas Mark 7

1 Halve each capsicum, keeping the stalk intact. Remove the seeds and membrane. Drizzle with olive oil, place cut side up on a roasting tray and roast in the oven for 20 minutes, until tender. Remove and leave to cool. Any juices gathered in the capsicum you can add to the stuffing mix.

2 Heat the olive oil in a frying pan over a medium heat. Add the onion then stir and fry for 4 minutes, until pale and soft. Remove from the heat.

3 Next, make the pearl couscous. Cook the pearl couscous in boiling water for 8-10 minutes, or according to packet directions. Drain. Transfer to a bowl.

4 To the pearl couscous add the cooked onions, corn kernels, avocado, tomato, pine nuts, mint flakes and lemon juice. Stir to combine. Season to taste with salt and freshly ground black pepper. Spoon the mixture into the cooked capsicums and serve.

~ Makes 6 ~

Rice cubes

This recipe uses a rice cube to form the rice into neat, perfectly formed cubes. Feel free to use your favourite risotto recipe, but make sure your ingredients are finely chopped. If you cannot get hold of a rice cube, roll the mixture into bite-size balls.

3 cups / 750ml vegetable stock
2 tablespoons olive oil
1 onion, peeled and chopped
1 garlic, peeled and crushed
1 cup / 200g Arborio rice
½ cup / 100g chargrilled capsicum strips, finely chopped
¼ cup / 50g sun-dried tomatoes, finely chopped
Freshly ground black pepper

1 Prepare the stock and place in a saucepan over a low heat to keep warm.

2 Heat the olive oil in a large frying pan over a medium heat. Add the onion and fry for 4 minutes, until pale and soft. Add the garlic and cook for a further minute. Add the rice and stir constantly for another minute, coating the rice in the oil.

3 Ladle ½ cup of stock into the pan, stirring constantly. Once the stock has absorbed, add another ladleful, stirring the rice as you go. Continue in this way, waiting for the stock to absorb before adding more. By the time you have used all the stock, your rice will be thick and creamy. This process will take about 20 minutes.

4 Stir in the chargrilled capsicum and sun-dried tomatoes and cook for another minute. Season well with freshly ground black pepper.

5 Take your rice cube and spoon the risotto into the cube, following the instructions carefully as you go. Place each completed cube on a serving plate. Best served at room temperature.

~ **Makes about 18** ~

Tabbouleh in mini pitas

Depending on the size of your pita bread, you can halve or quarter them to make small pockets for filling with your tabbouleh. You could also make a garlic sauce to go with them; just use the recipe for potatoes in garlic sauce.

½ cup / 100g bulghar wheat
1 tablespoon olive oil
1 onion, peeled and chopped
2 tomatoes, seeded and chopped
1 clove garlic, peeled and crushed
2 tablespoons chopped fresh parsley
1 teaspoon dried mint flakes
1 teaspoon ground cumin
Juice of 1 lemon
1 tablespoon extra virgin olive oil
Salt and freshly ground black pepper
2 pita breads

1 Place the bulghar wheat in a bowl and cover with cold water. Leave to soak for 30 minutes and then drain thoroughly into a sieve.

2 Meanwhile, heat the olive oil in a frying pan over a medium heat. Add the onion and cook for 4 minutes, until pale and soft. Place in a bowl.

3 To the onions, add the tomatoes, garlic, parsley, mint and cumin. When the bulghar wheat is ready, add it to the bowl along with the lemon juice and extra virgin olive oil. Mix well. Season to taste with salt and freshly ground black pepper. You can leave to stand to allow the flavours to develop.

4 Cut the pitas into 4 to form 4 pockets. Fill each pita pocket with the tabbouleh and serve.

~ Makes 8 ~

Capsicums stuffed with spiced bulghar

Roasting the capsicums first gives them a lovely flavour. However, be careful to not overcook them as you want them to retain their shape for stuffing.

---

3 red or green capsicums
2 tablespoons olive oil, plus extra for drizzling
1 cup / 200g bulghar wheat
2½ cups / 625ml vegetable stock
1 onion, peeled and chopped
1 clove garlic, peeled and crushed
1 tomato, chopped
1 teaspoon ground cinnamon
1 teaspoon ground cumin
1 teaspoon ground coriander
1 tablespoon lemon juice
Salt and freshly ground black pepper

Preheat the oven to 210°C / 410°F / Gas Mark 7

1 Halve each capsicum, keeping the stalk intact. Remove the seeds and membrane. Drizzle with olive oil, place cut side up on a roasting tray and roast in the oven for 20 minutes, until tender. Remove from the oven, then leave to cool.

2 Next, prepare the bulghar wheat. Place the bulghar wheat and vegetable stock in a medium saucepan and bring to the boil. Lower the heat, then simmer gently until the stock has absorbed. This will take about 10 minutes. Remove from the heat and fluff up with a fork.

3 Whilst the bulghar wheat is cooking, heat the 2 tablespoons of olive oil in a frying pan over a medium heat. Add the onion and garlic and fry for 4 minutes, until pale and soft. Remove from the heat and place in a bowl with the cooked bulghar wheat.

4 To the bulghar wheat and onions, add the tomato, cinnamon, cumin, coriander and lemon juice. Mix thoroughly. Season to taste with salt and freshly ground black pepper. Spoon the mixture into the cooked capsicums. Serve.

~ Makes 6 ~

Stuffed onion shells

Rather than presenting your guests with a whole stuffed onion to work their way through, you can offer them these delicate morsels. Boiling the onions softens them and loses some of the strong flavour.

2 large onions
1 cup / 200g long grain rice
1 tablespoon olive oil
150g Swiss brown mushrooms, finely chopped
1 clove garlic, peeled and crushed
1 teaspoon dried thyme
1 teaspoon dried oregano
¼ cup / 35g pine nuts

1 Peel the onions and cut off the root. Cut in half, making sure to cut through the root end. Bring a large saucepan of water to the boil. Add the onions and boil for 5 minutes. Drain. You may need to do this in batches, depending on the size of your saucepan. Pull apart the layers of the onions.

2 Cook the rice according to packet directions.

3 Heat the olive oil in a large frying pan over a medium heat. Add the mushrooms, garlic, thyme, oregano and pine nuts. Cook for 5 minutes, stirring often. Remove from the heat then add to the rice, stirring well to combine.

4 Use a teaspoon to fill the onion layers. For the larger layers, fold the onion over the rice to enclose it. You can use cocktail sticks to hold them in place. Serve warm or cold.

~ Makes about 24 ~

Italian sushi

Okay. It's Italian sushi because it's made using risotto. It also includes sun-dried tomato and chargrilled capsicum so some good flavours here. It's then rolled up in a nori sheet – so you will need a sushi mat to assist you.

1 tablespoon olive oil
1 onion, peeled and chopped
1 clove garlic, peeled and crushed
½ cup / 100g Arborio rice
1½ cups / 375ml vegetable stock
1 tablespoon savoury yeast flakes
Freshly ground black pepper

2 nori sheets
2 tablespoons sun-dried tomato strips
2 tablespoons chargrilled capsicum strips

1 Heat the olive oil in a medium saucepan over a medium heat. Add the onion and fry for 4 minutes, until pale and soft. Add the garlic and fry for another minute. Add the rice, stirring for 1 minute until the rice is thoroughly coated with the oil.

2 Add ½ cup of vegetable stock and stir until the stock has absorbed. Continue adding the stock, stirring until you have used all the stock and the rice is creamy and cooked. Stir in the savoury yeast flakes and season to taste with freshly ground black pepper. Leave to cool for 10 minutes.

3 Lay a nori sheet on a sushi mat, shiny side down. Spoon half of the risotto over the nori, spreading evenly. Leave a 2cm gap at the end furthest from you. Place 1 tablespoon each of sun-dried tomato strips and capsicum strips across the centre of the rice. Brush the end with water, then use the sushi mat to carefully roll up the nori. Repeat with the remaining risotto, tomato and capsicum. Slice each sushi into 6, arrange on a plate and serve.

~ **Makes 12** ~

Tomatoes stuffed with couscous

This stuffing recipe is quick to prepare as the only ingredient you need to cook is the onion. The couscous cooks itself and the rest is simply chopped. Since the tomatoes are not cooked, try to get the best quality tomatoes. Truss are good.

1 tablespoon olive oil
1 onion, peeled and chopped
1 tablespoon balsamic vinegar
1 tablespoon brown sugar
½ cup / 50g couscous
½ cup / 125ml boiling water
100g marinated tofu, cut into small cubes
1 tablespoon chopped fresh parsley
1 teaspoon dried chives
Salt and freshly ground black pepper
5 medium truss tomatoes
Extra virgin olive oil, for drizzling

1 Heat the olive oil in a frying pan over a medium heat. Add the onion then cook until pale and soft, about 4 minutes. Add the balsamic vinegar and brown sugar and mix well into the onions. Cook for another 5 minutes, until the onions are caramelised. Remove from the heat.

2 Bring a kettle of water to the boil. Place the couscous in a bowl and add the boiling water. Let it stand for 5 minutes. Fluff up with a fork to separate the grains.

3 Add the onions to the couscous, together with the tofu, parsley and chives. Season to taste with salt and freshly ground black pepper.

4 Cut the tomatoes in half, through the stalk end. Scoop out the seeds. Season with salt and pepper and then add the stuffing. Just before serving, drizzle with a small amount of extra virgin olive oil.

~ Makes 10 ~

Risotto balls

You will need to prepare the risotto in advance as it needs to be cold to form balls. You can use your favourite risotto recipe here, just make sure your vegetables are finely chopped.

3 cups / 750ml vegetable stock
2 tablespoons olive oil
1 onion, peeled and chopped
1 garlic, peeled and crushed
1 cup / 200g Arborio rice
2 large tomatoes, seeded and chopped

4 tablespoons chopped fresh parsley
Freshly ground black pepper
½ cup / 125ml soy milk
1 cup / 140g dried bread crumbs
3 tablespoons canola oil

1 Prepare the stock and place in a saucepan over a low heat to keep warm.

2 Heat the olive oil in a large frying pan over a medium heat. Add the onion and fry for 4 minutes, until pale and soft. Add the garlic and cook for a further minute. Add the rice and stir constantly for another minute, coating the rice in the oil.

3 Ladle ½ cup of stock into the pan, stirring constantly. Once the stock has absorbed, add another ladleful, stirring the rice as you go. Continue in this way, waiting for the stock to absorb before adding more. By the time you have used all the stock, your rice will be thick and creamy. This process will take about 20 minutes.

4 Stir in the tomatoes and parsley and cook for another minute. Season well with freshly ground black pepper. Spoon into a bowl, then leave to cool before refrigerating to chill the rice.

5 Place the milk in a bowl and the bread crumbs on a plate. Take tablespoons of the rice mixture and use your hands to form balls. Coat the balls in the milk and then roll in the bread crumbs.

6 Heat the canola oil in a large frying pan over a medium heat. Add the balls and fry for 6 minutes, until golden, turning often. Serve warm.

~ Makes 24 ~

Tomatoes stuffed with herbed rice

Feel free to use any combination of fresh herbs for the stuffing. Rosemary, mint and basil would all work well.

½ cup / 100g long grain rice
1 tablespoon chopped fresh thyme
1 tablespoon chopped fresh parsley
1 tablespoon chopped fresh oregano
1 tablespoon savoury yeast flakes
1 tablespoon lemon juice
1 tablespoon extra virgin olive oil
Salt and freshly ground black pepper
4 tomatoes

1 Cook the rice, according to packet directions. Fluff up with a fork. Stir in the thyme, parsley, oregano, savoury yeast flakes, lemon juice and extra virgin olive oil. Season to taste with salt and freshly ground black pepper.

2 Cut the tomatoes in half through the stalk and scoop out the seeds. Season with salt and freshly ground black pepper. Fill with the prepared rice. Serve.

~ Makes 8 ~

Falafel

For these falafel, do not worry about trying to make neat rounds as you spoon the mixture into the pan. This is homemade food after all and they contrast nicely to the dry packaged falafel you can sometimes end up with. Goes well with minty cream dip.

400g can chickpeas, rinsed and drained
1 small onion, peeled and chopped
1 clove garlic, peeled and crushed
½ teaspoon ground cumin
½ teaspoon ground coriander
½ teaspoon dried mint flakes
½ teaspoon ground turmeric
½ teaspoon caraway seeds
1 teaspoon lemon juice
½ cup / 75g plain flour
4 tablespoons canola oil

---

1 To a food processor, add the chickpeas, onion, garlic, cumin, coriander, mint flakes, turmeric, caraway seeds and lemon juice. Process until the mixture is well combined. Add the flour, blending it thoroughly into the mixture until it all comes together.

2 Heat the canola oil in a large frying pan over a medium heat. Add rounded tablespoons of the mixture to the pan and flatten slightly. Fry for 6-8 minutes, until golden brown all over. Use tongs to help you turn them. Drain on paper towel. Serve warm or cold.

~ Makes 12 ~

Mini bean patties

No pre-cooking is needed to prepare these patties. The ingredients are blitzed up in the food processor and then baked in the oven. Enjoy these patties with sweet chilli sauce.

1 small onion, peeled and coarsely chopped
1 clove garlic, peeled and crushed
125g button mushrooms, coarsely chopped
400g can kidney beans, rinsed and drained
1 tablespoon tomato paste
1 teaspoon dried chilli flakes
½ teaspoon smoked paprika
¼ cup / 40g plain flour
Salt and freshly ground black pepper

Preheat the oven to 180°C / 350°F / Gas Mark 4

1 Place the onion, garlic, mushrooms, kidney beans, tomato paste, chilli flakes and paprika into a food processor. Process until the mixture comes together. The mixture should be chunky but well combined. Stir in the flour and season with salt and freshly ground black pepper.

2 Line a baking tray with baking paper. Place heaped tablespoons of the mixture onto the baking tray. Press down slightly with the back of a spoon to form patties.

3 Bake the patties in the oven for 25 minutes, until firm and cooked. Leave to cool for 5 minutes, before transferring to a serving plate. Serve.

~ Makes 16 ~

Spiced chickpeas

These are very quick and simple to make. You could serve these as an alternative to nuts.

400g can chickpeas, rinsed and drained
1 tablespoon olive oil
1 teaspoon fennel seeds
1 teaspoon smoked paprika
½ teaspoon chilli powder
1 teaspoon sea salt flakes

Preheat the oven to 200°C / 400°F / Gas Mark 6

1 Place the drained chickpeas in a bowl. Add the olive oil, fennel seeds, smoked paprika and chilli powder. Mix thoroughly until the chickpeas are thoroughly coated with the flavourings.

2 Spread the chickpeas onto a baking tray lined with baking paper. Bake for 10 minutes. Remove from the oven. Sprinkle with the sea salt flakes before transferring to a serving bowl. Serve warm or cold.

~ Makes 2 cups ~

Lentil cakes

These melt-in-the-mouth lentil cakes are given a flavour boost with mushrooms, spices and cashews. I have used Swiss brown mushrooms; feel free to choose your favourite variety. You may like to serve these with a topping of chilli jam.

1 tablespoon olive oil
1 onion, peeled and chopped
1 clove garlic, peeled and crushed
120g Swiss brown mushrooms, sliced
2 slices wholegrain bread
400g can lentils, rinsed and drained
2 tablespoons unroasted cashews
1 tablespoon tomato paste
1 teaspoon ground turmeric
1 teaspoon ground cumin

Salt and freshly ground black pepper
3 tablespoons canola oil

1 Heat the olive oil in a large frying pan over a medium heat. Add the onion and fry for 4 minutes, until pale and soft. Add the garlic and mushrooms and fry for another 4 minutes, until the mushrooms are soft. Remove from the heat.

2 In a food processor, blitz up the slices of bread to form crumbs. Add the mushrooms and onions, lentils, cashews, tomato paste, turmeric and cumin. Process until the mixture is smooth like a paste and well combined. Season to taste with salt and freshly ground black pepper.

3 Heat the canola oil in a large frying pan over a medium heat. Add tablespoonfuls of the lentil mixture to the pan. Fry for 4 minutes, until golden on one side. Turn and fry for another 2 minutes. You will need to do this in batches and you may need to add more canola oil to the pan. Drain on paper towel. Serve.

~ Makes 20 ~

Chickpea bites

You can make these chickpea bites in advance. However, they are best served warm, so reheat them on a baking tray in a 200°C / 400°F / Gas Mark 6 oven for 10 minutes.

1 tablespoon olive oil
1 onion, peeled and chopped
400g can chickpeas, rinsed and drained
1 clove garlic, peeled and crushed
1 teaspoon lemon juice
2 tablespoons chopped fresh coriander
1 teaspoon ground cumin
¼ cup / 40g plain flour
Salt and freshly ground black pepper
3 tablespoons canola oil

1 Heat the olive oil in a frying pan over a medium heat. Add the onion then fry for 4 minutes, until pale and soft. Remove from the heat.

2 In a food processor, combine the onion, chickpeas, garlic, lemon juice, coriander and cumin. Process until the mixture is well combined. Mix in the flour and season with salt and freshly ground black pepper. Take level tablespoons of the mixture and form into balls.

3 Heat the canola oil in a large frying pan over a medium heat. Add half of the balls, pressing down slightly as you do so. Fry for 3 minutes, until golden on one side. Turn, then fry for another 2 minutes. Drain on paper towel. Repeat for the remaining balls. Serve.

~ **Makes 14** ~

Bean and herb mini sausages

These sausages are full of flavour and go superbly with mayonnaise or aioli. If the mixture seems slightly wet, you can add some corn flour to make it more manageable.

400g can butter beans
1 tablespoon canola oil
1 teaspoon liquid smoke
1 tablespoon chopped fresh parsley
1 teaspoon dried thyme
1 teaspoon dried sage
1 teaspoon onion powder

¼ cup / 35g dried bread crumbs
Salt and freshly ground black pepper
Canola oil, for brushing

Preheat the oven to 200°C / 400°F / Gas Mark 6

1 Place the butter beans in a food processor along with the canola oil, liquid smoke, parsley, thyme, sage and onion powder. Process until the mixture is well combined.

2 Take tablespoons of the mixture and use your hands to form sausages. Roll the sausages in the dried bread crumbs, seasoned with salt and freshly ground black pepper. Place the sausages on a baking tray and brush with canola oil. Bake for 15 minutes until golden and cooked. Leave to cool before serving.

~ Makes 12 ~

Spicy roasted nuts

The nice thing about creating your own flavoured nuts is you can choose what goes in them. These nuts contain no salt, yet are full of flavour. They are good served warm.

1 tablespoon olive oil
1 teaspoon brown sugar
1 teaspoon ground cumin
1 teaspoon ground coriander
¼ teaspoon chilli powder
½ cup / 75g unroasted cashews
½ cup / 75g blanched almonds

Preheat the oven to 170°C / 325°F / Gas Mark 3

1 In a bowl, mix together the olive oil, sugar, cumin, coriander and chilli powder. Add the cashews and almonds and mix well until the nuts are thoroughly coated.

2 Spread the nuts on a baking tray lined with baking paper. Place in the oven and roast for 15 minutes. Leave to cool for a few minutes on the tray before transferring to a serving bowl. Serve warm or cold.

~ **Makes 1 cup** ~

Herby nuts

I have used unroasted macadamias and cashews for this nut recipe. You can use any nut you like, just make sure it is unroasted.

1 tablespoon olive oil
1 teaspoon dried rosemary
1 teaspoon dried thyme
1 teaspoon dried oregano
½ teaspoon garlic powder
Freshly ground black pepper
½ cup / 75g unroasted macadamias
½ cup / 75g unroasted cashews

Preheat the oven to 170°C / 325°F / Gas Mark 3

1 In a bowl mix together the olive oil, rosemary, thyme, oregano, garlic powder and a good grind of black pepper. Add the macadamias and cashews and stir well to coat the nuts.

2 Tip the nuts onto a baking tray lined with baking paper. Bake for 15 minutes, until golden and fragrant. Transfer to a serving bowl. Can be served warm or cold.

~ Makes 1 cup ~

Nutty balls

You can use whatever nuts you fancy for this recipe; it is a good way to use up leftovers. You can also choose your preferred stuffing mix; just remember to check that it is vegan friendly first.

85g pack stuffing mix
1 tablespoon olive oil
1 small onion, peeled and chopped
1 clove garlic, peeled and crushed
½ cup / 75g nuts, finely chopped

Preheat the oven to 210°C / 410°F / Gas Mark 7

1 Make up the stuffing according to packet directions. Leave to stand until it is cool enough to handle.

2 Meanwhile, heat the olive oil in a frying pan over a medium heat. Add the onion and garlic and fry for 4 minutes, until pale and soft.

3 To the stuffing, add the onions and chopped nuts. Stir well to combine. Use your hands to form balls. Place on a baking tray. Bake in the oven for 20 minutes, until crispy. Serve warm.

~ Makes 14 ~

POTATOES

Puffed potato slices

These fried potatoes are simple yet moreish. When returning the potatoes to the pan on a high heat, you do not need to add more oil as the potatoes will cook in the oil that is already on them. You can prepare these in advance, up to the end of step 3. When ready, reheat in a 200°C / 400°F / Gas Mark 6 oven on a baking tray for 10 minutes, then sprinkle with salt, pepper and rosemary.

450g potatoes
4 tablespoons canola oil
Sea salt flakes
1 teaspoon dried rosemary
Freshly ground black pepper

1 Peel and thinly slice the potatoes about 5mm thick. Pat dry with paper towel.

2 Heat the canola oil in a large frying pan over a medium heat. Add the potatoes without overlapping. You will have to do this in batches. Fry for 4 minutes, turning once. Drain on paper towel.

3 Turn the heat up and return the potatoes to the pan. Cook until the potatoes are golden and puffed, about 2 minutes. Drain on paper towel.

4 Transfer to a serving plate and sprinkle with sea salt flakes, rosemary and plenty of freshly ground black pepper. Serve.

~ **Makes about 30** ~

Baby hasselbacks

Hasselback potatoes are simple to prepare and a joy to eat. Just take care when cutting the potatoes so as not to cut all the way through. This is why I suggest you use chopsticks to help you.

8 baby potatoes, peeled
3 tablespoons canola oil
Finely grated peel of 1 lemon
1 teaspoon dried sage
1 teaspoon dried thyme
1 teaspoon dried rosemary
Freshly ground black pepper
Sea salt flakes

Preheat the oven to 190°C / 375°F / Gas Mark 5

1 Place a chopstick on either side of a potato. Make even-sized cuts into the potato, about 5mm apart. Make sure you do not cut all the way through; the chopsticks will help prevent this. Repeat for all of the potatoes. Place in a roasting tin.

2 In a small bowl or jar, mix together the canola oil, lemon peel, sage, thyme, rosemary and a good grind of black pepper. Pour the oil over the potatoes, making sure they are evenly coated. Roast in the oven for about 50 minutes, until crisp on the outside and tender on the inside.

3 Place on a serving plate and sprinkle with sea salt flakes. Serve.

~ Makes 8 ~

Patatas bravas

Patatas bravas are a classic tapas dish, great for sharing. Serve in a large bowl so guests can help themselves.

450g potatoes, peeled and cut into 2cm cubes
2 tablespoons olive oil
1 onion, peeled and chopped
1 clove garlic, peeled and crushed
400g can chopped tomatoes
1 tablespoon red wine vinegar
1 teaspoon chilli powder
1 teaspoon smoked paprika
Salt and freshly ground black pepper

---

1 Bring lightly salted water to the boil in a large saucepan. Add the potatoes, bring back to the boil and parboil for 5 minutes. Drain and set aside.

2 Heat the olive oil in a large frying pan over a medium heat. Add the onion and garlic and fry for 4 minutes, until pale and soft. Add the chopped tomatoes, red wine vinegar, chilli powder and paprika. Cook for 2 minutes, stirring.

3 Add the potatoes, stirring them into the mixture. Season with salt and pepper. Turn the heat down slightly and cover the pan. Simmer for 15 minutes, removing the lid for the last 5. Cook until the potatoes are tender and the juices have cooked down. Serve in a large bowl.

~ Makes 2 cups ~

Crispy baked potato skins

Although you could bake the potatoes in the oven first, it is much quicker to microwave them and the results are just as good. I have given instructions for both methods.

4 large potatoes, scrubbed
Canola oil, for brushing
Sea salt flakes
Freshly ground black pepper

Preheat the oven to 200°C / 400°F / Gas Mark 6

1 Prick the potatoes. Place in the oven and bake for around 50 minutes, until tender. Alternatively you can microwave the pricked potatoes on high for around 10 minutes, depending on the size of the potatoes and the power of your microwave. Again, cook until tender. Leave to stand until they are cool enough to handle.

2 Cut the potatoes into quarters. Scoop the flesh out of each quarter, using a metal spoon. Your skins should be about 5mm thick. Place the skins on a baking tray and brush both sides with canola oil. Season liberally with sea salt flakes and freshly ground black pepper. Bake for 30 minutes, turning once, until crisp. Serve with a dip of your choice.

~ **Makes 16** ~

Mediterranean potato shells

You will get plenty of filling for this recipe. However, I think it is far better to pile high the flavours rather than have rations.

4 large potatoes, scrubbed
2 tablespoons olive oil
1 onion, peeled and chopped
1 clove garlic, peeled and crushed
150g mushrooms, coarsely chopped
2 tomatoes, chopped

¼ cup / 40g pitted black olives, sliced
¼ cup / 35g pine nuts, toasted
1 tablespoon savoury yeast flakes
½ teaspoon dried marjoram
½ teaspoon dried oregano
Salt and freshly ground black pepper

Preheat the oven to 200°C / 400°F / Gas Mark 6

1 Prick the potatoes and bake in the oven for 50 minutes, until tender. Alternatively microwave the pricked potatoes on a high power for 10 minutes. Times will vary according to the power of your oven and size of the potatoes. Let stand until the potatoes are cool enough to handle.

2 Halve the potatoes and using a metal spoon, scoop out the flesh leaving 1cm's worth to form a shell for your filling. Place on a baking tray.

3 To make the filling, heat the olive oil in a large frying pan over a medium heat. Add the onion and fry for 4 minutes, until pale and soft. Add the garlic and mushrooms and fry for a further 5 minutes, until the mushrooms are soft and golden. Remove from the heat and tip into a bowl.

4 To the bowl add the tomatoes, olives, pine nuts, savoury yeast flakes, marjoram and oregano. Mix together, season to taste with salt and black pepper, then spoon into the prepared potato shells. Bake in the oven for 15 minutes, until heated through. Serve warm.

~ Makes 8 ~

Potatoes in garlic sauce

This recipe is very garlicky, which in my opinion is what makes it so good. However if you are worried about the amount of garlic used, you can easily make the sauce with just 2 cloves of garlic.

450g potatoes, peeled and cut into 2cm cubes
4 tablespoons canola oil

For the sauce:
2 tablespoons canola oil
2 tablespoons plain flour
1¼ cup / 300ml soy milk
3 cloves garlic, peeled and crushed
1 tablespoon chopped fresh parsley
½ tablespoon savoury yeast flakes
Salt and freshly ground black pepper

1 Bring a large saucepan of lightly salted water to the boil. Add the potatoes, bring the water back to the boil and then boil for 10 minutes, until tender. Drain.

2 Heat the canola oil in a large frying pan over a medium-high heat. Add the potatoes and fry, turning often, until golden. This will take about 8-10 minutes. Drain on paper towel. Place in a serving bowl. Cover with a plate to keep warm whilst you make the sauce.

3 To make the garlic sauce, warm the canola oil in a small saucepan. In a small cup, mix the flour with some of the milk to form a smooth, thin paste. Add the paste to the oil, stirring well to combine. Gradually add the rest of the milk, stirring well with a wooden spoon. Bring to the boil. Once it is boiling, reduce the heat and simmer for 5 minutes, until it starts to thicken, still stirring. Once it has started to thicken, stir in the garlic, parsley, savoury yeast flakes, a pinch of salt and a good grind of black pepper. Stir until thick, about 3-4 minutes.

4 Pour the sauce over the potatoes, stirring carefully to ensure the potatoes are covered with the sauce. Serve.

~ Makes 2 cups ~

Spiced potato wedges

Homemade potato wedges are really simple to make. These wedges are oven-baked, making them healthier than fried versions, but you will still end up with crisp, golden wedges.

2 large potatoes, scrubbed
2 tablespoons canola oil
1 teaspoon smoked paprika
1 teaspoon ground cumin
1 teaspoon garlic powder
Freshly ground black pepper

Preheat the oven to 210°C / 410°F / Gas Mark 7

1 Halve each potato, then cut each half into 4, making 16 wedges in total. Place the potatoes in a bowl.

2 To the bowl add the canola oil, smoked paprika, ground cumin, garlic powder and a good grind of black pepper. Mix thoroughly to coat the potatoes.

3 Place the potatoes on a lined baking tray. Bake in the oven for 25 minutes. Remove from the oven and turn the potatoes. Return to the oven for another 20 minutes, until the wedges are crisp and golden on the outside and tender on the inside. Serve.

~ **Makes 16** ~

Herby potato cakes

You can use your favourite herbs for these potato cakes. Use whatever is in season, or whatever you prefer.

900g potatoes, peeled
2 tablespoons soy milk
1 tablespoon chopped fresh basil
1 tablespoon chopped fresh chives
1 tablespoon chopped fresh parsley
2 spring onions, finely chopped
½ teaspoon garlic powder
Freshly ground black pepper
2 tablespoons olive oil

1 Cut the potatoes into even-sized pieces and place in a large saucepan of lightly salted water. Bring to the boil, reduce the heat very slightly and simmer until the potatoes are tender. This will take about 20 minutes, but will depend on the size of your potato pieces. You can test the potatoes with a knife; it should go in easily. Drain.

2 Place the potatoes in a large bowl, then mash until smooth. Add the soy milk and the basil, chives and parsley. Add the spring onions and garlic powder and a good grind of black pepper. Mix thoroughly. Once the potato is cool enough to easily handle, take heaped tablespoons of the potato and roll into balls, then flatten to form cakes.

3 Heat the olive oil in a large frying pan over a medium heat. Add the potato cakes and fry for 4 minutes. Carefully turn them, then fry for another 3 minutes, until golden. Serve warm.

~ Makes 14 ~

Cheesy stuffed potatoes

Crunchy on the outside, creamy on the inside, your guests are sure to love these potatoes. In summer you can finish the potatoes off on the barbecue rather than in the oven.

8 baby potatoes, scrubbed
70g vegan cream cheese
1 tablespoon olive oil
½ teaspoon dried rosemary
½ teaspoon salt
½ teaspoon freshly ground black pepper

1 Prick the potatoes then place in a large saucepan and cover with water. Bring to the boil and cook for about 20 minutes, until the potatoes are tender. Drain.

Preheat the oven to 200°C / 400°F / Gas Mark 6

2 Once the potatoes are cool enough to handle, use an apple corer to make a hole in each potato, taking care not to go through the bottom. Using a teaspoon, fill each potato with the cream cheese.

3 In a small bowl, mix together the olive oil, rosemary, salt and black pepper. Brush the potatoes with the oil then place on a baking tray. Bake in the oven for 30 minutes, until the skins are crispy. Serve warm or cold.

~ Makes 8 ~

Sweet potato fries

Although you could use regular potatoes for this recipe, the spices go particularly well with sweet potato. If you do use regular potatoes, you will need to bake them for longer.

2 sweet potatoes, about 700g in total
2 tablespoons olive oil
1 clove garlic, peeled and crushed
1 teaspoon cumin seeds
Whole nutmeg

Preheat the oven to 200°C / 400°F / Gas Mark 6

1 Peel the sweet potatoes. Slice into fries about 1cm thick and 10cm long. Place in a bowl. To the bowl add the olive oil, garlic, cumin seeds and a good grating of nutmeg. Coat the potatoes evenly with the flavours. Turn out onto a baking tray. Bake for 20 minutes, turn the potatoes then bake for another 15 minutes, until tender and cooked. Serve with a dip of your choice.

~ **Makes about 50 fries** ~

Roast potatoes

Roast potatoes in their simplest form are probably one of my favourite foods. Since this is tapas, baby potatoes are used so they can be kept whole. I find the easiest way to turn roasties is to use two teaspoons.

12 baby potatoes
Canola oil
Salt and freshly ground black pepper

Preheat the oven to 200°C / 400°F / Gas Mark 6

1 Peel the potatoes and put them in a saucepan of cold water. Bring to the boil, then turn the heat down slightly. Parboil for 8 minutes. Drain.

2 Meanwhile, add enough canola oil to cover the bottom of a roasting tin. Heat the oil in the oven for 10 minutes. Remove from the oven, tip in the potatoes and season with salt and freshly ground black pepper.

3 Roast in the oven for 25 minutes. Remove the tin from the oven and turn the potatoes. Return to the oven and roast for another 25 minutes. By this time the potatoes will be golden and crunchy. Drain on paper towel before transferring to a serving dish. Serve.

~ **Makes 12** ~

Bombay potatoes

The spicy flavours in this recipe will linger on the palate long after you have taken your last bite.

500g potatoes, peeled and cut into 2cm cubes
3 tablespoons canola oil
1 clove garlic, peeled and crushed
1 teaspoon mustard seeds
1 teaspoon fennel seeds
1 teaspoon ground turmeric
1 teaspoon ground coriander
1 teaspoon ground cumin
2 tablespoons chopped fresh coriander
Salt and freshly ground black pepper

---

1 Bring a large saucepan of lightly salted water to the boil. Add the potatoes then parboil for 5 minutes. Drain.

2 Heat the canola oil in a large frying pan over a medium heat. Add the garlic, mustard seeds, fennel seeds, turmeric, coriander and cumin. Fry for 1 minute stirring the spices into the oil. Add the potatoes, stirring well so the potatoes are covered in the spicy oil. Cover the pan and lower the heat.

3 Cook for 15 minutes, stirring every 5 minutes or so. The potatoes should be tender and golden. Remove from the heat and stir through the fresh coriander. Season to taste with salt and black pepper. Tip into your choice of serving bowl. Serve warm.

~ Makes 2 cups ~

Let's call them Scotch eggs

There's no egg or meat in these Scotch eggs, but they do look like Scotch eggs and they do taste good. I've used Vegemeal sausage mix for ease – use your preferred brand or even create your own.

450g potatoes
Salt and freshly ground black pepper
½ teaspoon onion powder
½ teaspoon ground turmeric
3 x 110g packs Vegemeal vegetable sausage mix
½ cup / 70g dried bread crumbs
Canola oil, for deep-frying

1 Prepare the mash. Peel the potatoes and cut into small chunks. Place in a saucepan of lightly salted water and bring to the boil. Turn down the heat slightly and simmer for about 15 minutes, until tender. Drain. Return the potatoes to the pan. Mash. Season well with salt and black pepper and stir in the onion powder.

2 Scoop 5 teaspoons of the potato into a small bowl. Add the turmeric, mixing well to evenly colour the potato. Roll a teaspoon of the potato into a ball. Repeat to make 5 in total. Place on a baking paper lined plate and freeze for 15 minutes.

3 Once the balls of potato are frozen, knead the remaining potato, then slice into 5 even pieces. Lay the pieces out on your work surface. Taking one frozen ball at a time, place the ball in the middle of the potato and gather the mash up around it. Shape into a ball or oval. Repeat for the remaining potato. Freeze the potato on a baking paper lined plate for at least an hour.

4 Make up the packs of Vegemeal according to packet instructions. Divide into 5 even amounts. Place the dried bread crumbs in a bowl. Taking one potato at a time, coat it in the Vegemeal mix, forming a ball, then roll in the bread crumbs.

4 Half-fill a large saucepan with the canola oil and heat over a medium heat. Use a slotted spoon to lower the balls into the oil and fry until golden, about 6 minutes. Drain on paper towel. Leave to cool for a few minutes and then slice into halves or quarters. Serve warm or cold.

~ Makes 10 halves ~

BREAD, POLENTA AND FRITTERS

Pita crisps

You can prepare these pita crisps in advance as they are fine eaten cold.

---

1 teaspoon cumin seeds
1 teaspoon ground coriander
1 teaspoon sesame seeds
Salt and freshly ground black pepper
2 pita breads
Olive oil, for brushing

Preheat the oven to 200°C / 400°F / Gas Mark 6

1 In a small bowl, mix together the cumin seeds, coriander, sesame seeds, a pinch of salt and a grind of black pepper.

2 Brush the pita breads with olive oil. Distribute the spice mix across the two pitas. Slice into 3cm strips. A pizza cutter works well for this.

3 Place on a baking tray and bake in the oven for 10 minutes, until crisp.

4 Leave to cool, then serve with your choice of dip.

~ Makes 16 ~

Melba toasts

These Melba toasts are great for topping as well as dipping. If you have white bread, you can quickly make these as it is the only ingredient you need.

4 slices white bread

Preheat the grill

1 Place the bread on a wire grill tray and cook under the grill until lightly toasted. Turn and toast the other side. Remove from the grill.

2 Using a serrated knife, cut off the crusts. Next, carefully cut each slice of bread in half as though you were splitting a muffin. A sawing motion helps. You will end up with 8 thin squares. Cut each square in half using a sharp knife, to make 16 rectangles.

3 Place rectangles back on the wire grill tray, untoasted side up. Place under the grill and cook until golden. Leave to cool. Serve.

~ **Makes 16** ~

Tortilla dippers

Easy to prepare, these spicy dippers make the perfect accompaniment to a dip of your choice.

2 flour tortillas
Olive oil, for brushing
1 teaspoon smoked paprika
1 teaspoon chilli powder
½ teaspoon garlic powder

Preheat the oven to 200°C / 400°F / Gas Mark 6

1 Cut each tortilla in half, then quarters. Then cut each quarter into 3 triangles. This will make 24 triangles in total. A pizza cutter works well here.

2 Brush each triangle with olive oil and place on a baking tray. Sprinkle the paprika, chilli and garlic powder evenly over each triangle.

3 Place in the oven and bake for 10 minutes, until crisp. Remove from the oven and leave to cool before serving.

~ **Makes 24** ~

Tortilla dippers version 2

*When I am creating recipes, I sometimes do variations and choose a favourite.
After serving up this recipe, my taster insisted I keep both versions; so here it is.*

2 flour tortillas
Olive oil, for brushing
1 teaspoon fennel seeds
1 teaspoon dried chilli flakes
1 teaspoon ground coriander

Preheat the oven to 200°C / 400°F / Gas Mark 6

1 Cut each tortilla in half, then quarters. Then cut each quarter into 3 triangles. This will make 24 triangles in total. A pizza cutter works well here.

2 Brush each triangle with olive oil and place on a baking tray. Sprinkle the fennel seeds, chilli flakes and coriander evenly over each triangle.

3 Place in the oven and bake for 10 minutes, until crisp. Remove from the oven and leave to cool before serving.

~ Makes 24 ~

Crostini

Just one ingredient is all that is needed for this recipe. It only requires half a baguette, so if you have any left over from the day before, feel free to use it.

½ baguette

Preheat the oven to 200°C / 400°F / Gas Mark 6

1 Thinly slice the baguette into 1cm rounds. Place on a baking tray and bake until crisp and brown, turning once. This will take about 10-12 minutes. Serve with a topping of your choice.

~ **Makes about 16** ~

Bruschetta

Thick slices of bread flavoured with garlic and olive oil, what could be better? Don't underestimate the impact merely rubbing a clove of garlic on the bread has. It really does flavour the bread. I have used a baguette for this recipe, you can also use ciabatta if you prefer.

1 white baguette
1 clove garlic, peeled
2 teaspoons extra virgin olive oil

Preheat the grill

1 With a serrated knife, slice the baguette on an angle, about 2.5cm thick.

2 Place the bread on a wire grill tray and toast until golden about 1-2 minutes on each side. Remove from the grill.

3 Rub the garlic clove over the bread, then brush with olive oil. Serve with a topping of your choice.

~ Makes about 16 ~

Grissini

Do you remember as a child rolling sausage shapes from plasticine? Turns out you were learning a skill that would enable you to make perfect grissini (breadsticks). Making homemade grissini is easy to do with the help of your electric mixer. You can mix the dough by hand; it will just take more time.

1 cup / 250ml water
3 cups / 450g plain flour
2 tablespoons olive oil
1 teaspoon granulated sugar
2½ teaspoons instant dried yeast
1 teaspoon salt
2 tablespoons finely chopped fresh parsley
2 teaspoons sea salt flakes

1 To an electric mixer with a dough hook, add the water, flour, olive oil, sugar and yeast. Mix until the dough starts to come together. Add the salt and parsley. Continue mixing to form a dough. To test readiness, the dough should spring back when pressed. Alternatively, you can use a breadmaker on the dough setting, adding the ingredients according to manufacturer's instructions.

2 Put the dough in a large bowl, cover with plastic wrap then stand in a warm place for 1 hour. It should have doubled in size.

3 Remove the dough from the bowl and give it a punch to knock it back. Using a sharp knife, divide the dough into 16 even-sized pieces. Roll each piece into a long thin stick, at least 30cm long. Place on to 2 floured baking trays, leaving space between each breadstick. Cover with a tea towel. Stand in a warm place for 30 minutes.

Preheat the oven to 220°C / 425°F / Gas Mark 7

4 Remove the tea towel and sprinkle the sticks with sea salt flakes. Bake in the oven for 12-15 minutes, until the grissini are golden brown. Serve warm or cold.

~ Makes 16 ~

Spiced flatbread

Don't worry about your flatbreads being perfectly round; they'll stand in impressive contrast to mass produced goods that you could have served up.

1⅓ cups / 200g plain flour
1⅓ cups / 200g wholemeal flour
1 teaspoon chilli powder
1 teaspoon ground cumin
1 teaspoon onion powder
1 teaspoon garlic powder
Freshly ground black pepper
1¼ cups / 300ml water
Olive oil spray

1 In a large bowl or food processor, add the flours, chilli, cumin, onion powder, garlic powder and a good grind of black pepper. Gradually add the water then mix well until a dough forms.

2 Tip the dough onto a floured work surface then knead until it is smooth. Using a sharp knife, cut the dough into 14 even-sized pieces. Roll into balls, then flatten into rounds no more than 5mm thick. Spray with olive oil.

3 Heat a large frying pan over a medium-high heat. Add the dough rounds and cook for about 2 minutes on each side until golden and puffed. Transfer to a serving plate. Can be served warm or cold with a dip or topping of your choice.

~ Makes 14 ~

Mini wraps

Flour tortillas are filled, rolled and sliced to make bite-size pieces. None of the ingredients are cooked, so it is quick to prepare. You will need to pop the wraps into the fridge for a few hours to firm up however.

400g can kidney beans, rinsed and drained
100g Swiss brown mushrooms
2 sun-dried tomatoes
2 teaspoons lime juice
Tabasco sauce
2 large flour tortillas
2 spring onions, finely chopped

1 In a food processor, add the kidney beans, mushrooms, sun-dried tomatoes, lime juice and a few drops of Tabasco sauce. Process until the mixture is smooth and well combined.

2 Take a flour tortilla and spread half of the kidney bean mixture over it, using a metal spoon. Sprinkle with half of the spring onions. Repeat for the other tortilla.

3 Starting from the end nearest you, firmly roll up the tortillas. Cover each wrap in plastic wrap then refrigerate for 2 hours.

4 Remove the plastic wrap, trim the ends and then slice each wrap into 8 even-sized pieces. Serve.

~ Makes 16 ~

Polenta wedges

These polenta wedges make a tasty base for your favourite topping. They go particularly well with roasted tomatoes and olives.

3⅔ cups / 900ml vegetable stock
1½ cups / 225g polenta
2 tablespoons extra virgin olive oil
½ teaspoon garlic powder
½ teaspoon onion powder
Freshly ground black pepper
Olive oil, for brushing

1 Bring the vegetable stock to the boil in a medium non-stick saucepan. Once boiling, gradually add the polenta, stirring constantly with a wooden spoon. Reduce the heat and continue stirring the polenta until it has thickened. This will take about 10 minutes.

2 Remove from the heat and add the olive oil, garlic powder and onion powder and a good grind of black pepper, stirring quickly to combine. Pour the mixture into a 20 x 30cm oiled baking tin. Use the back of a spoon to spread the mixture evenly, making sure to get into the corners. Leave to cool, then place in the refrigerator to firm up. Allow a couple of hours.

Preheat the grill

3 Remove the polenta from the tin and using a large, sharp knife cut the polenta into 12 squares. Brush with olive oil. Place on a wire grill tray and grill for about 10 minutes on each side until golden and crisp. Serve warm with your choice of topping.

~ Makes 12 ~

Herby polenta slices

For this polenta recipe, I cut the cooked polenta into diamond shapes for added interest. The best way to do this is cut from corner to corner, to form a cross. Using these cuts as a guide, continue cutting about 4cm apart. You will have triangles left over for you to enjoy as a snack.

3⅔ cups / 900ml vegetable stock
1½ cups / 225g polenta
2 tablespoons extra virgin olive oil
2 tablespoons chopped fresh basil
2 tablespoons chopped fresh parsley
2 tablespoons chopped fresh mint
½ teaspoon garlic powder
Freshly ground black pepper
Olive oil, for brushing

1 Bring the vegetable stock to the boil in a medium non-stick saucepan. Once boiling, gradually add the polenta, stirring constantly with a wooden spoon. Reduce the heat and continue stirring the polenta until it has thickened. This will take about 10 minutes.

2 Remove from the heat and add the olive oil, basil, parsley, mint, garlic powder and a good grind of black pepper, stirring quickly to combine. Pour the mixture into a 20 x 30cm oiled baking tin. Use the back of a spoon to spread the mixture evenly, making sure to get into the corners. Leave to cool, then place in the refrigerator to firm up. Allow a couple of hours.

Preheat the grill

3 Remove the polenta from the tin and using a large, sharp knife cut the polenta into diamond shapes. Brush with olive oil. Place on a wire grill tray and grill for about 10 minutes on each side until golden and crisp. Serve warm with your choice of topping.

~ Makes 12 ~

Polenta fingers

This is another way to serve polenta. By cutting them into fingers, you can serve them with a dip of your choice. Expect these to be eaten quickly.

1 teaspoon yeast extract
3⅔ cups / 900ml vegetable stock
1½ cups / 225g polenta
2 tablespoons extra virgin olive oil
½ teaspoon garlic powder
½ teaspoon onion powder
Freshly ground black pepper
1 clove garlic, peeled and crushed
2 tablespoons olive oil

1 Stir the yeast extract into the vegetable stock. Bring the vegetable stock to the boil in a medium non-stick saucepan. Once boiling, gradually add the polenta, stirring constantly with a wooden spoon. Reduce the heat and continue stirring the polenta until it has thickened. This will take about 10 minutes.

2 Remove from the heat and add the extra virgin olive oil, garlic powder, onion powder and a good grind of black pepper, stirring quickly to combine. Pour the mixture into a 20 x 30cm oiled baking tin. Use the back of a spoon to spread the mixture evenly, making sure to get into the corners. Leave to cool, then place in a refrigerator to firm up. Allow a couple of hours.

Preheat the grill

3 Remove the polenta from the tin and using a large, sharp knife cut the polenta into fingers. Begin by cutting the polenta lengthwise to make two 10 x 30cm rectangles. Then cut each rectangle into fingers about 2cm thick. Mix the garlic with the olive oil, then brush it over the polenta. Place on a wire grill tray and grill for about 8 minutes on each side until golden and crisp. Leave to cool for about 10 minutes and serve with your choice of dip.

~ Makes 24 ~

Chilli and onion polenta slices

I've given this polenta a flavour boost with two types of onion and some chilli powder. Like any of the polenta recipes, you can slice into fingers or squares depending on whether you are using them for topping or dipping.

1 tablespoon olive oil
1 onion, peeled and chopped
1 red onion, peeled and chopped
3⅔ cups / 900ml vegetable stock
1½ cups / 225g polenta
2 tablespoons extra virgin olive oil
1 teaspoon garlic powder
½ teaspoon chilli powder
Freshly ground black pepper
Olive oil, for brushing

1 Heat the olive oil in a frying pan over a medium heat. Add both onions and fry for 6 minutes, until pale and soft. Remove from the heat.

2 Bring the vegetable stock to the boil in a medium non-stick saucepan. Once boiling, gradually add the polenta, stirring constantly with a wooden spoon. Reduce the heat and continue stirring the polenta until it has thickened. This will take about 10 minutes.

3 Remove from the heat and add the onions, extra virgin olive oil, garlic powder, chilli powder and a good grind of black pepper, stirring quickly to combine. Pour the mixture into a 20 x 30cm oiled baking tin. Use the back of a spoon to spread the mixture evenly, making sure to get into the corners. Leave to cool, then place in a refrigerator to firm up. Allow a couple of hours.

Preheat the grill

4 Remove the polenta from the tin and using a large, sharp knife cut the polenta into 12 squares. Brush with olive oil. Place on a wire grill tray and grill for about 8 minutes on each side until crispy. Serve warm.

~ Makes 12 ~

Gorditas

Gorditas are a Mexican stuffed cornmeal cake. Because of their size, they are perfect for tapas. You can vary the filling to suit.

1 cup / 150g polenta
1 cup / 150g plain flour
1 teaspoon baking powder
½ teaspoon salt
1 tablespoon canola oil
2 cups / 500ml hot water
4 tablespoons canola oil, for frying

For the filling:
1 tablespoon olive oil
4 mushrooms, diced
400g can kidney beans, rinsed and drained
1 tomato, chopped
½ teaspoon smoked paprika

1 In a large bowl, mix together the polenta, flour, baking powder and salt. Add 1 tablespoon of canola oil and the water. Mix together with a wooden spoon, until the mixture comes together. Turn the mixture out onto a floured work surface and then divide into 12 even-sized balls. Using floured hands, flatten the balls to make 8cm sized rounds.

2 Heat a large frying pan over a medium heat. Add the rounds and cook for 3-4 minutes, until they start to brown. Turn and cook for another 2-3 minutes. Remove from the pan.

3 Wipe down the pan and add 4 tablespoons of canola oil. Heat the oil over a medium heat. Return the gorditas to the pan and fry for 3 minutes, until golden. Turn, then fry for another 2 minutes. Drain on paper towel.

4 To make the filling, heat the olive oil in a medium saucepan over a medium heat. Add the mushrooms and cook until soft, about 5 minutes. Add the kidney beans and mash slightly. Heat through for 3-4 minutes. Remove from the heat and stir in the tomato and smoked paprika.

5 Use a sharp knife to carefully split open the gorditas to make a pocket as you would with a pita bread. Fill with spoonfuls of the mushroom and bean mixture. Serve.

~ Makes 12 ~

Onion bhaji

These onion bhaji are made with plain flour and work really well. However, for a more authentic flavour replace the plain flour with chickpea flour.

½ cup / 75g plain flour
1 teaspoon baking powder
½ teaspoon ground cumin
½ teaspoon ground coriander
½ teaspoon chilli powder
¼ teaspoon ground turmeric
1 teaspoon canola oil
100ml water
1 clove garlic, peeled and crushed
2 onions, peeled and chopped
Canola oil, for frying

1 First make the batter. In a bowl mix together the flour, baking powder, cumin, coriander, chilli powder and turmeric. Add the canola oil and water and mix thoroughly to make a smooth batter. Stir in the garlic and onions, making sure they are well coated with the batter.

2 Place enough oil into a deep-sided frying pan or wok so it is about 1cm deep. Heat on a medium setting. Once the oil is hot, add tablespoons of the mixture to the pan, leaving space between each bhaji. Fry for about 5-6 minutes, until brown and crispy. You may need to turn them if the oil does not fully coat them. Drain on paper towel. Serve.

~ Makes 16 ~

Corn fritters

These fritters go nicely with sweet chilli sauce. However you can serve them with a topping of your choice. Something with tomatoes would go well, or try chilli jam or avocado cream.

⅓ cup / 50g wholemeal self-raising flour
310g can corn kernels, drained
3 spring onions, chopped
1 teaspoon ground coriander
½ teaspoon chilli powder
1 tablespoon lime juice
⅓ cup / 80ml soy milk
1 teaspoon canola oil
2 tablespoons canola oil, for frying

1 In a bowl add the flour, corn kernels, spring onions, coriander, chilli powder, lime juice, soy milk and 1 teaspoon of canola oil. Stir well to combine all the ingredients together.

2 Heat 2 tablespoons of canola oil in a large frying pan over a medium heat. Spoon heaped tablespoons of the batter into the pan. Flatten slightly to form fritters. Fry for 3 minutes, turn and cook for another 1-2 minutes, until browned on both sides. Drain on paper towel. Serve.

~ **Makes 10** ~

Artichoke fritters

This is a simple yet flavoursome fritter recipe that uses artichoke hearts. I use canned artichokes; however feel free to use a jar of marinated artichoke hearts. These can be prepared in advance then reheated on a baking tray at 200°C / 400°F / Gas Mark 6 for 10 minutes.

⅓ cup / 50g self-raising flour
400g can artichoke hearts, drained and chopped
1 teaspoon dried oregano
1 clove garlic, peeled and crushed
⅓ cup / 80ml soy milk
1 tablespoon lemon juice
1 teaspoon canola oil
Freshly ground black pepper
2 tablespoons canola oil, for frying

1 In a bowl, mix together the self-raising flour, artichoke hearts, oregano, garlic, milk, lemon juice and 1 teaspoon of canola oil. Season well with freshly ground black pepper. Mix to make a batter.

2 Heat the canola oil in a large frying pan over a medium heat. Add heaped tablespoons of the mixture to the pan, pressing down to form fritters. Fry for 3 minutes, until brown. Turn and cook for another 2 minutes. Drain on paper towel. Serve warm.

~ Makes 10 ~

Zucchini and capsicum fritters

Juicy zucchini and crunchy capsicum are combined together into a tasty bite-size fritter. Both are cubed, so the mixture will be lumpy. Don't worry though it will come together as a fritter with the help of flour and milk. You can cook these in advance then reheat on a baking tray at 200°C / 400°F / Gas Mark 6 for 10 minutes.

1 zucchini (about 200g), chopped into 1cm cubes
1 red capsicum (about 200g), chopped into 1cm pieces
⅓ cup / 50g self-raising flour
⅓ cup / 80ml soy milk
1 tablespoon chopped fresh parsley
1 teaspoon lemon juice
Salt and freshly ground black pepper
2 tablespoons canola oil

1 Mix together in a large bowl the zucchini, capsicum, flour, milk, parsley and lemon juice. Season with salt and freshly ground black pepper. Make sure the flour is thoroughly mixed in and the zucchini and capsicum are well coated.

2 Heat the canola oil in a large frying pan over a medium heat. Add heaped tablespoons of the mixture to the pan, then press down with a spatula. Fry for 3 minutes then turn and fry for another 1-2 minutes, until golden on both sides. Drain on paper towel. Serve warm.

~ **Makes 10** ~

Blini

Blini are a type of pancake that uses yeast as its raising agent rather than self-raising flour. I have used a combination of wholemeal and plain flour for this recipe. You could replace the wholemeal flour with buckwheat flour, if you prefer.

60g silken tofu
½ tablespoon lemon juice
⅔ cup / 160ml soy milk
½ cup / 75g plain flour
½ cup / 75g wholemeal plain flour
2 teaspoons bicarbonate of soda
1 teaspoon granulated sugar
1 teaspoon instant dried yeast
½ teaspoon salt
1 tablespoon canola oil

1 Place the tofu and lemon juice in a food processor and process until smooth. Pour into a saucepan and add the milk. Warm gently over a low heat for 2 minutes, stirring to combine. Remove from the heat.

2 Combine the flours with the bicarbonate of soda, sugar and yeast in a large bowl. Beat in the milk and tofu mixture then add the salt. Make sure the mixture is smooth and free from lumps. Cover the bowl with plastic wrap or a tea towel and leave to stand for an hour.

3 After an hour, remove the plastic wrap and give the mixture a brief stir.

4 Heat a large frying pan over a medium-high heat. Brush the pan with canola oil then add tablespoonfuls of the blini mixture. Cook for 2 minutes until golden, turn, then cook for another minute. Transfer to a plate. You will need to cook the blini in batches, so remember to brush the pan with oil each time, before adding the batter. Serve with a topping of your choice.

~ Makes 18 ~

PASTRIES AND BISCUITS

Pizza tarts

This recipe makes 9 pizza tarts and uses squares of pastry pressed into the holes of a muffin tin. The squares give a more rustic look to the tarts, although if you prefer you can always cut the pastry into rounds.

1 tablespoon olive oil
1 onion, peeled and chopped
1 red capsicum, seeded and chopped into 1cm pieces
1 clove garlic, peeled and crushed
75g button mushrooms, sliced
1 teaspoon dried oregano
1 tablespoon chopped fresh basil
3 tablespoons grated vegan mozzarella-style cheese
Salt and freshly ground black pepper
1 sheet frozen puff pastry, thawed
1 tomato, sliced

Preheat the oven to 200°C / 400°F / Gas Mark 6

1 Heat the olive oil in a frying pan over a medium heat. Add the onion and fry for 4 minutes, until soft. Add the capsicum, garlic and mushrooms and fry for another 3 minutes, until the vegetables are soft. Remove from the heat.

2 Stir in the oregano, basil and mozzarella-style cheese. Season to taste with salt and black pepper.

3 Cut the pastry into 9 even-sized squares. Press each square into a hole of a muffin tin. No need to be too precise and it is okay for the corners to stick up.

4 Top the pastry squares with the mixture. Top each with a slice of tomato and finish with a grind of black pepper. Place in the oven and cook for 30 minutes, until the pastry is golden. Leave to cool for 5 minutes before removing from the muffin tin. Serve warm.

~ **Makes 9** ~

Galettes

Galettes are rounds or squares of pastry that are given a topping. I have deliberately kept these galettes simple so you can add your own choice of toppings.

1 sheet frozen puff pastry, thawed
½ tablespoon soy milk

Preheat the oven to 180°C / 350°F / Gas Mark 4

1 Cut the pastry into 12 even-sized rectangles. Place on a baking tray lined with baking paper and prick the rectangles all over with a fork.

2 Cover the rectangles with another sheet of baking paper and place another baking tray on top. Place in the oven and bake for 10 minutes.

3 Remove from the oven and take off the top baking tray and sheet of baking paper. Brush the pastry with the milk.

4 Return to the oven and bake for another 10 minutes, until golden. Leave to cool then serve with your choice of toppings.

~ **Makes 12** ~

Baked samosas

Baking rather than deep-frying the samosas cuts down on the fat content in this recipe. To help you make the pastry rounds, you could use a saucer as a template.

300g potatoes, peeled and chopped into cubes
100g frozen peas
2 tablespoons canola oil
1 onion, peeled and chopped
2 teaspoons chopped fresh ginger
1 clove garlic, peeled and crushed
1 green chilli, seeds removed and chopped
2 teaspoons mild curry paste
3 sheets frozen shortcrust pastry, thawed
1 tablespoon soy milk

Preheat the oven to 180°C / 350°F / Gas Mark 4

1 Bring a saucepan of lightly salted water to the boil. Add the potatoes and boil for 5 minutes. Add the peas and continue cooking until the potatoes are tender, about another 5 minutes. Drain.

2 Heat the canola oil in a large frying pan. Add the onion and cook until soft, about 5 minutes. Add the ginger, garlic, green chilli and curry paste. Cook and stir for another 2 minutes before adding the potatoes and peas. Give a good stir, making sure the potato is thoroughly coated in the spicy mixture. Remove from the heat. Finally, using a potato masher, mash the mixture, ensuring you are left with no big lumps of potato.

3 Cut 4 x 12cm rounds from each sheet of pastry. Cut each round in half to make semi-circles. Add a teaspoonful of mixture to one half of the semi-circle. Fold the pastry over and press down the edges to encase the mixture. Using a fork will help seal the pastry and give a decorative finish. Brush with the milk. Place on a baking tray and bake in the oven for 30 minutes, until golden. Serve warm.

~ Makes 24 ~

Golden bites

These tasty bites are made using a choux-style pastry. I have used a blue-style cheese, but you can use your favourite. The vegan cream cheese and sage topping finishes them off fantastically.

1 tablespoon golden flaxmeal
3 tablespoons warm water
40g vegan margarine
½ cup / 125ml water
½ cup / 75g plain flour
Freshly ground black pepper
1 tablespoon
½ cup / 50g grated vegan blue-style cheese
60g vegan cream cheese
½ teaspoon dried sage

Preheat the oven to 200°C / 400°F / Gas Mark 6

1 Place the flaxmeal and 3 tablespoons of warm water in a food processor and blitz until combined and thick. Leave to stand for 10 minutes.

2 In a small saucepan add the margarine and water. Bring to the boil. Once it is boiling, reduce the heat then add the flour and a good grind of black pepper, beating quickly with a wooden spoon. Do this until the mixture comes away from the side of the pan, about 1 minute. Remove from the heat. Beat in the flaxmeal, followed by the blue-style cheese.

3 Take heaped teaspoonfuls of the mixture and spoon onto a lined baking tray. Place in the oven and bake for 30 minutes, until lightly golden.

4 Leave to cool on a wire rack. Once cool, top the bites with a small dollop of cream cheese and a few flecks of sage. Serve.

~ Makes 20 ~

Caramelised onion quiches

Caramelising the onions give an abundance of flavour to these quiches. It does not take long to do and the results are worthwhile.

2 tablespoons olive oil
1 onion, peeled and sliced
1 tablespoon balsamic vinegar
1 tablespoon brown sugar
300g firm tofu
¼ cup / 60ml soy milk
1 tablespoon lemon juice
2 tablespoons savoury yeast flakes
1 teaspoon dried thyme
Salt and freshly ground black pepper
1 sheet frozen puff pastry, thawed

Preheat the oven to 200°C / 400°F / Gas Mark 6

1 Heat the olive oil in a frying pan over a low heat. Add the onion and fry for 4 minutes, until pale and soft. Add the vinegar and sugar and cook, stirring for another 10 minutes, until caramelised. Remove from the heat.

2 In a food processor, blitz together the tofu, milk, lemon juice, savoury yeast flakes and thyme. Season with a pinch of salt and a good grind of black pepper.

3 Cut the pastry sheet into 9 equal squares or rounds, then line the holes of a muffin tin with the pastry.

4 Spoon the onions over the pastry. Top with the tofu mixture. Place in the oven and bake for 30-35 minutes, until risen and golden. Leave to stand for 10 minutes before removing the quiches from the muffin tin. Serve warm or cold.

~ **Makes** 9 ~

Onion tarts

I use vegan cream cheese to add an additional flavour and texture to these tarts. The creaminess goes perfectly with the fried onions.

1 tablespoon olive oil
2 onions, peeled and sliced
1 clove garlic, peeled and crushed
125g vegan cream cheese
½ teaspoon dried sage
Freshly ground black pepper
2 sheets frozen puff pastry, thawed

Preheat the oven to 220°C / 425°F / Gas Mark 7

1 Heat the olive oil in a frying pan over a medium heat. Add the onions and garlic and fry for 8-10 minutes, until they start to brown. Remove from the heat.

2 In a small bowl, mix the cream cheese with the sage and a good grind of black pepper.

3 Using a 10cm pastry cutter, cut 8 rounds from the pastry. Press the rounds into a muffin tin.

4 Spoon the cream cheese evenly over the pastry, then top with the onions. Bake for 20 minutes, until the pastry is golden. Leave to cool for 5 minutes before transferring to a wire rack to cool. Serve at room temperature or cold.

~ **Makes 8** ~

Savoury twists

I use double pastry to make these twists nice and puffy. I have chosen to make 10 long twists, but you could easily cut the pastry in half to make 20. Serve with your choice of dip.

1 teaspoon caraway seeds
1 teaspoon dried oregano
1 teaspoon garlic powder
1 teaspoon onion powder
Freshly ground black pepper
1 teaspoon yeast extract
2 sheets frozen puff pastry, thawed
1 tablespoon soy milk

Preheat the oven to 220°C / 425°F / Gas Mark 7

1 In a small bowl, mix together the caraway seeds, oregano, garlic powder and onion powder. Season well with freshly ground black pepper.

2 Evenly spread the yeast extract over 1 sheet of pastry. Sprinkle on the spicy mixture, making sure to go to the edges. Place the second sheet of pastry over the mixture, pressing down firmly. You can use a rolling pin for this.

3 Brush the pastry with milk. Cut the pastry into 2cm strips. Taking each end, twist up the pastry and place on 2 lined baking trays. Bake for 15 minutes, until golden and crisp. Let stand for 5 minutes before transferring to a wire rack to cool. Serve.

~ Makes 10 ~

Tomato and mustard quiches

The combination of the two types of tomatoes with the Dijon mustard works really well. As with the other quiche recipes, I have used pastry squares. Use rounds if you prefer.

1 tomato, seeded and chopped
3 sun-dried tomatoes, chopped
300g firm tofu
¼ cup / 60ml soy milk
1 tablespoon lemon juice
1 tablespoon savoury yeast flakes
3 teaspoons Dijon mustard, divided
Salt and freshly ground black pepper
1 sheet frozen puff pastry, thawed
1 teaspoon chopped fresh parsley

Preheat the oven to 200°C / 400°F / Gas Mark 6

1 Combine the tomatoes and sun-dried tomatoes in a bowl. Season with freshly ground black pepper.

2 In a food processor, blitz together the tofu, milk, lemon juice, savoury yeast flakes and 1 teaspoon of Dijon mustard. Season with a pinch of salt and a good grind of black pepper.

3 Cut your puff pastry into 9 even-sized squares and press each square into the holes of a muffin tin. Spread the base of each pastry square with the remaining 2 teaspoons of Dijon mustard. Distribute the tomatoes evenly over the mustard then spoon on the tofu mixture. Bake in the oven for 30 minutes, until the quiches are golden and puffed. Remove from the oven and transfer to a wire rack to cool. Just before serving, sprinkle with the chopped parsley. Can be served warm or cold.

~ **Makes 9** ~

Spring rolls

Baking, rather than frying, cuts down on the fat content of these spring rolls. However, you can deep-fry them in a wok if you wish. Use canola or sunflower oil and fry until golden. If you cannot get hold of spring roll pastry, you can always use filo pastry.

1 cup / 40g rice vermicelli
1 small carrot, peeled and grated
2 spring onions, chopped
1 cup / 60g cabbage, finely chopped
1 clove garlic, peeled and crushed
1 teaspoon grated fresh ginger
1 tablespoon soy sauce
1 teaspoon sesame oil
12 sheets spring roll pastry
Olive oil, for brushing

Preheat the oven to 200°C / 400°F / Gas Mark 6

1 Cook the rice vermicelli according to packet directions. Drain thoroughly and roughly chop. Add to a bowl with the carrot, spring onions, cabbage, garlic and ginger. Stir in the soy sauce and sesame oil.

2 Take one sheet of spring roll pastry and spoon a tablespoonful of the mixture into one corner and then fold the corner over the mixture. Brush olive oil over the other corners. Fold in the two sides, then roll the pastry up. Place seam side down on a baking tray. Repeat with the rest of the mixture. Brush the prepared spring rolls with some more oil.

3 Bake in the oven for about 20 minutes, until golden. Serve warm or cold with a dip of your choice.

~ Makes 12 ~

Tofu and cranberry puffs

This is a very simple recipe that you can put together in minutes. Even if you are not having a tapas party, they are a nice snack on their own.

2 sheets frozen puff pastry, thawed
¼ cup / 60g cranberry sauce
160g firm tofu, drained and sliced
½ tablespoon savoury yeast flakes
¼ teaspoon garlic powder
¼ teaspoon onion powder
Soy milk, for brushing

Preheat the oven to 200°C / 400°F / Gas Mark 6

1 Cut each sheet of pastry into 4 even-sized squares. Spoon the cranberry sauce into the middle of each square, spreading it evenly. Mix together the savoury yeast flakes, garlic powder and onion powder. Coat the tofu slices in the mixture. Place the tofu on top of the cranberry sauce. Be sure to leave plenty of room to fold your pastry corners inwards.

2 Fold the corners of the pastry square into the middle. Brush with soy milk. Place on a baking tray and bake for 20 minutes, until crisp and golden. Serve warm or cold.

~ **Makes 8** ~

Empanadas

Empanadas are a stuffed Spanish pastry. Traditionally they are fried, but I have baked them for this recipe.

1 tablespoon olive oil
1 onion, peeled and chopped
1 clove garlic, peeled and crushed
150g firm tofu
1 teaspoon dried thyme
Pinch of chilli powder
Salt and freshly ground black pepper
2 sheets frozen shortcrust pastry, thawed
Soy milk, for brushing

Preheat the oven to 200°C / 400°F / Gas Mark 6

1 Heat the olive oil in a frying pan over a medium heat. Add the onion and garlic and fry for 5 minutes, until slightly golden. Remove from the heat.

2 In a small bowl, mash the tofu with a fork. Add the onions, thyme and chilli powder. Mix well to combine and season to taste.

3 Using a 10cm round cookie cutter, cut 4 rounds from each sheet of pastry. Re-roll the remaining pastry and cut 4 more rounds to make 12 in total.

4 Spoon a heaped teaspoonful of the tofu mixture onto one half of a pastry round. Fold over and press the sides together firmly to seal. Brush with milk and place on a baking tray. Repeat for all the rounds. Bake in the oven for 25 minutes, until golden and crisp. Serve warm or cold.

~ Makes 12 ~

Herby tomato tarts

Drizzling herb oil over these freshly baked tomato tarts makes them particularly delicious and flavoursome. The herb oil would also be lovely drizzled over polenta wedges.

1 sheet frozen puff pastry, thawed
1 teaspoon savoury yeast flakes
2 tomatoes, thinly sliced
Salt and freshly ground black pepper

For the herb oil:
1 tablespoon chopped fresh basil
1 tablespoon chopped fresh parsley
1 teaspoon dried oregano
3 tablespoons extra virgin olive oil

Preheat the oven to 220°C / 425°F / Gas Mark 7

1 Cut the pastry into 9 even-sized squares. Place on a lined baking tray then score around the edge of each, 1cm in.

2 Sprinkle the pastry squares with the savoury yeast flakes, then top with a slice or 2 of tomato. Season with salt and freshly ground black pepper. Bake in the oven for about 18 minutes, until the pastry is golden and puffed.

3 In a jar or small bowl, mix together the basil, parsley, oregano and extra virgin olive oil. Just before serving, drizzle a small amount of the oil over each tart.

~ Makes 9 ~

Spanakopita

Spanakopitas are Greek filo pastries filled with cheese and spinach. For this recipe I have used tofu instead of cheese and to save time (and energy) I have used wanton wrappers instead of filo. If you cannot get hold of wanton wrappers, feel free to use filo pastry or even shortcrust or puff pastry.

1 tablespoon olive oil
1 onion, peeled and chopped
3 cups / 150g baby spinach
100g firm tofu, drained and diced into small cubes
150g silken tofu
Whole nutmeg
Salt and freshly ground black pepper
26 fresh wanton wrappers (250g pack)
Water, for brushing
Soy milk, for glazing

Preheat the oven to 200°C / 400°F / Gas Mark 6

1 Heat the olive oil in a large frying pan over a medium heat. Add the onion and fry for 4 minutes, until pale and soft. Stir in the spinach and cook for 2 minutes, until the spinach has wilted. Remove from the heat and leave to cool for 5 minutes. Place in a bowl along with the diced tofu.

2 Put the silken tofu in a food processor and process until smooth and creamy. Season well. Stir into the spinach, onions and tofu. Add a good grating of nutmeg and season to taste with salt and freshly ground black pepper.

3 Lay out your wanton wrappers and place a heaped teaspoon of the mixture in the centre of each. Brush the edges of the wrapper with water and fold in half to form a triangle. Press the edges firmly together and place on a baking tray. Brush your pastries with milk. Bake in the oven for 20 minutes, until golden and starting to crisp around the edges. Serve warm.

~ Makes 26 ~

Olive and capsicum quiches

The creamy tofu and salty olives make a delightful combination in these quiches. If you have stuffed green olives, feel free to use them in this recipe.

1 sheet frozen puff pastry, thawed
300g firm tofu
¼ cup / 60ml soy milk
1 tablespoon lemon juice
1 tablespoon savoury yeast flakes
1 teaspoon dried chives
Salt and freshly ground black pepper
3 tablespoons chargrilled capsicum, chopped
18 green olives, pitted (about 60g)

Preheat the oven to 200°C / 400°F / Gas Mark 6

1 Cut the puff pastry into 9 even-sized squares and press each square into the holes of a muffin tin.

2 In a food processor, blitz together the tofu, milk, lemon juice, savoury yeast flakes and dried chives. Season with a pinch of salt and a good grind of black pepper.

3 Spoon the chopped capsicum into the base of each pastry square, followed by the tofu mixture. Cut the olives in half and add 4 halves to each quiche. Bake in the oven for 30-35 minutes, until the quiches are golden and puffed. Remove from the oven and transfer to a wire rack to cool. Can be served warm or cold.

~ Makes 9 ~

Baby spinach and tomato roulade

I've made this roulade using a sheet of puff pastry. The filling is spread on the pastry which is rolled up then baked until golden. Use a serrated knife to cut up the roulade.

For the filling:
1 tablespoon olive oil
1 onion, peeled and chopped
1 clove garlic, peeled and crushed
3 cups / 150g baby spinach
1 tomato, seeded and finely chopped
100g vegan cream cheese
Whole nutmeg
Salt and freshly ground black pepper

1 sheet frozen puff pastry, thawed
Soy milk, for brushing
½ teaspoon sesame seeds
½ teaspoon poppy seeds

Preheat the oven to 200°C / 400°F / Gas Mark 6

1 Heat the olive oil in a large frying pan over a medium heat. Add the onion and garlic and fry for 4 minutes, until pale and soft. Add the spinach, stirring through until it has wilted, about 2 minutes. Stir in the tomato and cream cheese, mixing well to melt the cheese. Remove from the heat. Grate on some nutmeg, then season to taste with salt and freshly ground black pepper.

2 Spread the filling evenly over the thawed sheet of pastry. Roll up the pastry then carefully transfer to a baking tray. Brush the pastry with milk and sprinkle with the sesame seeds and poppy seeds. Bake for 30 minutes until the pastry is golden and puffed. Leave to cool on the tray before slicing into 8. Serve.

~ Makes 8 slices ~

Cheesy biscuits

You can use your choice of vegan cheese for these biscuits. This recipe is very quick and you'll have tasty treats for your guests in no time.

½ cup / 75g plain flour
50g vegan margarine
½ cup / 50g grated vegan Parmesan-style cheese
½ tablespoon savoury yeast flakes
½ teaspoon mustard powder
Freshly ground black pepper

Preheat the oven to 200°C / 400°F / Gas Mark 6

1 To an electric mixer with a beater blade add the flour, margarine, Parmesan-style cheese, savoury yeast flakes, mustard powder and a good grind of black pepper. Process until the mixture forms a dough.

2 Tip the dough onto your work surface, then roll into a 15cm log. Slice into 20 even-sized discs, each about 5mm thick. Place on a lined baking tray.

3 Bake for 15 minutes, until the biscuits are firm and starting to brown around the edges. Transfer to a wire rack to cool. Serve.

~ **Makes 20** ~

Herb biscuits

Serve these biscuits on their own or with a topping of your choice. A good contrast would be chilli jam.

½ cup / 75g plain flour
50g vegan margarine
½ cup / 50g grated vegan cheddar-style cheese
1 tablespoon savoury yeast flakes
1 teaspoon dried oregano
1 teaspoon dried rosemary
1 tablespoon finely chopped fresh parsley
Freshly ground black pepper

Preheat the oven to 200°C / 400°F / Gas Mark 6

1 To an electric mixer with a beater blade add the flour, margarine, cheddar-style cheese, savoury yeast flakes, oregano, rosemary, parsley and a good grind of black pepper. Process until the mixture forms a dough.

2 Tip the dough onto your work surface, then roll into a 15cm log. Slice into 20 even-sized discs, each about 5mm thick. Place on a lined baking tray.

3 Bake for 15 minutes, until the biscuits are firm and starting to brown around the edges. Transfer to a wire rack to cool. Serve.

~ **Makes 20** ~

DESSERTS

Spicy cookies with orange cream

These cookies are a joy to eat when dipped in the orange cream. I came up with the orange cream recipe when I realised I had a peeled orange with nowhere to go. Less waste, more pleasure.

115g vegan margarine
¼ cup / 50g brown sugar
1 cup / 150g self-raising flour
1 teaspoon ground cinnamon
1 teaspoon freshly grated nutmeg
Finely grated peel of 1 orange
2 teaspoons Demerara sugar

For the orange cream:
125g vegan cream cheese
Juice of 1 orange
2 teaspoons caster sugar

Preheat the oven to 190°C / 375°F / Gas Mark 5

1 Place the margarine and sugar into a bowl and beat together until creamy. Add the flour, cinnamon, nutmeg and orange peel, mixing until a dough forms. You can do this in a food processor.

2 Place the dough on your work surface, then use your hands to form a log about 20cm long. Cut into 12 pieces.

3 Place each piece onto a lined baking tray, pressing down with the palm of your hand as you do so. They will be about 5cm in diameter. Try to leave space between each cookie as they will spread whilst cooking.

4 Sprinkle with Demerara sugar. Place in the oven and bake for 15 minutes, until golden. Stand for 10 minutes before transferring to a wire rack to cool. Serve with the orange cream.

5 To make the orange cream, beat the cream cheese with the orange juice and caster sugar in a small bowl. Spoon into a serving bowl.

~ **Makes 12 cookies** and ½ cup orange cream ~

Chocolate tarts

This recipe demonstrates the versatility of tofu. I have included instructions for blind baking the tart cases. However, if you prefer, use ready-made pastry cases. Doing so makes this a super-quick recipe.

2 sheets frozen shortcrust pastry, thawed
150g dark chocolate, broken into pieces
200g firm tofu, crumbled
¼ cup / 50g caster sugar
Icing sugar, for dusting

1 Using a 10cm pastry cutter, cut 4 rounds from each sheet of pastry. Re-roll the remaining pastry and cut an additional 4 rounds to make 12 in total. Press each round into the holes of a muffin tin, making sure the pastry goes up the sides. Prick all over. Refrigerate for 30 minutes to help prevent shrinkage.

Preheat the oven to 200°C / 400°F / Gas Mark 6

2 Place in the oven and cook for 10 minutes. Remove the tin from the oven and use the back of a teaspoon to press down on the pastry to remove any air pockets. Return to the oven and cook for another 10 minutes, until crisp and golden. Let the cases cool for a few minutes before transferring to a wire rack to cool completely.

3 Place the chocolate in a bowl over a saucepan of simmering water. Melt gently over a low heat, stirring until smooth. Remove from the heat.

4 Place the crumbled tofu and caster sugar in a food processor and process until the mixture is smooth. Add the tofu to the melted chocolate and stir well to combine. Spoon the mixture into the tart cases. Refrigerate until needed. Just before serving, dust with icing sugar.

~ Makes 12 ~

Mini doughnuts

These mini doughnuts are a fun addition to a tapas menu. They are baked rather than fried and use 2 mini doughnut tins. They work just as well in mini muffin tins if you cannot get hold of a doughnut tin.

1⅓ cup / 200g self-raising flour
½ cup / 100g granulated sugar
Pinch of salt
¾ cup / 180ml soy milk
2 teaspoons canola oil
½ teaspoon vanilla extract

For the icing:
1 cup / 125g icing sugar
2 tablespoons cocoa powder
1½ tablespoons soy milk

Preheat the oven to 220°C / 425°F / Gas Mark 7

1 Sift the flour into a bowl. Stir in the sugar and salt.

2 In a jug, beat together the milk, canola oil and vanilla extract. Add to the flour mixture and stir with a wooden spoon until the mixture is well combined.

3 Half-fill greased doughnut or muffin tins with the mixture. Bake for 8-9 minutes, until springy and puffed. You can check they are cooked by poking a cocktail stick in one of the doughnuts. It should come out clean. Let the doughnuts stand for 10 minutes before turning out onto a wire rack. Leave to cool completely before icing.

4 To ice the doughnuts, sift the icing sugar and cocoa powder into a small bowl. Add the milk, stirring until it is smooth. Using a spatula or metal spoon, spread the icing over each doughnut. Leave to set, before serving.

~ Makes 24 ~

Chocolate chip cookies

Use an electric mixer to quickly mix up some tasty cookie dough. I've made 12 fairly large cookies. You can always make the cookies smaller, but you may need to adjust the cooking time.

1 tablespoon golden flaxmeal
3 tablespoons warm water
125g vegan margarine
⅔ cup / 125g brown sugar
1½ cups / 225g self-raising flour
⅓ cup / 25g cocoa powder
1 cup / 160g vegan chocolate chips

Preheat the oven to 190°C / 375°F / Gas Mark 5

1 Place the flaxmeal and warm water in a food processor and blitz until combined and thick. Leave to stand for 10 minutes.

2 Place the margarine and sugar in a bowl and beat until creamy. Beat in the flaxmeal mixture. Next sift the flour and cocoa powder and fold into the mixture. Finally, stir in the chocolate chips. Knead the mixture into a dough. You can do all of this using an electric mixer with a beater blade.

3 Form the dough into a log. Using a sharp knife, slice the dough into 12. Take each slice and roll into a ball, then flatten slightly. Place on a lined baking tray. Bake in the oven for 15 minutes, until the cookies begin to firm around the edges. They will be soft when you first remove them, so let stand for 10 minutes before transferring to a wire rack to cool. Serve.

~ Makes 12 ~

Speedy banoffee pies

By using ready-made caramel, these banoffee pies are easily put together. Rather than one big pie, I use muffin cases for separate portions. You may like to offer guests a teaspoon for eating their pies.

180g digestive / wheatmeal biscuits
90g vegan margarine
2 bananas, peeled
¼ teaspoon ground cinnamon
340g can condensed caramel soymilke
200g vegan cream cheese
⅓ cup / 80ml coconut cream
1 teaspoon vanilla extract
1 tablespoon caster sugar
2 tablespoons desiccated coconut

1 Crush the biscuits until they are in crumbs. You can use a food processor for this or place the biscuits in a plastic bag and pound them with a rolling pin.

2 Melt the margarine in a small saucepan. Remove from the heat. Stir in the biscuits until they are thoroughly coated with the margarine. Line a 12-hole muffin tin with muffin cases and spoon the biscuit mixture evenly between the cases. Press down firmly with the back of a metal spoon.

3 Mash the bananas, using a fork. Stir in the cinnamon. Spoon the banana evenly over the biscuit bases.

4 Pour the caramel into a bowl and give it a stir. Spoon the caramel evenly over the bananas.

5 Using electric beaters, beat together the cream cheese, coconut cream, vanilla extract and caster sugar until thick. Spoon the cream over the caramel. Sprinkle the coconut over the cream. Refrigerate until you are ready to serve the pies. Remove the pies from the muffin tin and place on a plate. Serve.

~ Makes 12 ~

Apple cinnamon tarts

You can use any apple suitable for cooking in this recipe. Popular varieties include: Granny Smith, Royal Gala and Pink Lady (my favourite). The biscuits add a crumbly topping and you can choose your favourite variety here.

1 sheet frozen shortcrust pastry, thawed
2 apples (about 400g), peeled, cored and chopped
1 tablespoon granulated sugar
¼ teaspoon ground cinnamon
Whole nutmeg
½ cup / 125ml water
3 plain sweet biscuits

1 Cut the pastry into 9 squares. Line a muffin tin with each square, pressing down to form a tart case. You can trim the pastry into a round if you wish. Prick the pastry with a fork. Place the prepared pastry in the refrigerator for 30 minutes.

Preheat the oven to 200°C / 400°F / Gas Mark 6

2 Bake the pastry in the oven for 10 minutes. Remove from the oven. Press down on the pastry with the back of a teaspoon to remove any air pockets. Return to the oven for another 10 minutes, until the pastry is crisp and golden. Leave to cool for a few minutes before transferring to a wire rack. Leave to cool completely.

3 Put the apples in a medium sized saucepan with the sugar, cinnamon and a good grating of nutmeg. Add the water and bring to the boil. Cover, reduce the heat and simmer for 10 minutes, until the apples are cooked and soft.

4 Spoon the apples into the prepared cases. Crush the biscuits using a food processor or bash with a rolling pin until they are nicely crumbled. Sprinkle the biscuit crumbs over the tarts. Serve warm or cold.

~ **Makes 9** ~

Sugared twists

I use 2 sheets of pastry to make these twists, for extra puffiness. Don't worry too much about the sheets not sticking together when your press them down, as the twisting will hold them in place.

2 sheets frozen puff pastry, thawed
1 tablespoon soy milk
¼ cup / 50g brown sugar
1 teaspoon ground cinnamon
Whole nutmeg
Icing sugar, for dusting

Preheat the oven to 220°C / 425°F / Gas Mark 7

1 Brush one sheet of pastry with milk. Sprinkle on the brown sugar and cinnamon. Make sure you go to the edges. Add a good amount of grated nutmeg. Top with the other sheet of pastry and press down firmly to join the two sheets. Brush with more milk.

2 Cut the pastry into two rectangles. Then cut each rectangle into 2cm strips. Twist each strip, holding the strip at either end to help you. Place on to 2 lined baking trays and brush with some more milk.

3 Bake in the oven for 15 minutes, until golden and puffed. Cool on a wire rack then dust with icing sugar before serving.

~ **Makes 20** ~

Almond bites

These almond bites are quite sticky so make sure to use mini muffin cases so they don't end up sticking to the muffin tin.

½ cup / 125ml coconut cream
½ cup / 100g caster sugar
1 cup / 200g almond meal
2 tablespoons corn flour
1 teaspoon baking powder
1 teaspoon vanilla extract

Preheat the oven to 180°C / 350°F / Gas Mark 4

1 Put the coconut cream and sugar in a large bowl and beat with electric beaters until the mixture starts to thicken.

2 Using a wooden spoon, beat in the almond meal, corn flour, baking powder and vanilla extract.

3 Place mini muffin cases into a 12-hole mini muffin tin. Spoon the mixture evenly into the cases.

4 Bake in the oven for 25 minutes, until golden. Let them stand for 5-10 minutes, before transferring to a wire rack to cool. Serve.

~ Makes 12 ~

Cranberry and chocolate muffins

For a healthier version, you can use wholemeal self-raising flour instead of regular self-raising flour, or 1 cup of each. Use sunflower oil if you cannot find canola oil.

1 tablespoon golden flaxmeal
3 tablespoons warm water
2 cups / 300g self-raising flour
1 cup / 200g caster sugar
1 cup / 250ml soy milk
½ cup / 125ml canola oil
1 teaspoon almond essence
½ cup / 80g vegan chocolate chips
½ cup / 60g dried cranberries

Preheat the oven to 180°C / 350°F / Gas Mark 4

1 Place the flaxmeal and warm water in a food processor and blitz until combined and thick. Leave to stand for 10 minutes.

2 Line a 12-hole muffin tin with muffin cases.

3 In a large bowl, combine the flour and sugar. In a jug add the milk, oil, flaxmeal and almond essence. Beat together with a fork until well combined. Pour the liquid into the bowl and stir with a wooden spoon until just combined. Fold in the chocolate chips and dried cranberries.

4 Spoon the mixture evenly into the muffin cases. Place in the oven and bake for 30 minutes, until golden. The muffins should bounce back when pressed. Transfer to a wire rack to cool. Serve.

~ Makes 12 ~

Chocolate Julia

This is a no-cook chocolate cake based on Mary Berry's Chocolate Juliet recipe. I have named it Chocolate Julia as it is inspired by my favourite chocolate bars: fruit and nut and raisin and biscuit.

200g dark chocolate, broken into pieces
1 teaspoon vanilla extract
100g digestive / wheatmeal biscuits, roughly chopped
½ cup / 80g sultanas
½ cup / 75g blanched almonds, roughly chopped

1 Place the chocolate in a bowl over a saucepan of simmering water. Melt gently over a low heat, stirring until smooth. Remove from the heat.

2 Stir in the vanilla extract, biscuits, sultanas and almonds, making sure they are coated well with the chocolate.

3 Grease and line a 20cm square baking dish. Spoon in the mixture and press down with the back of a metal spoon. Chill in the refrigerator for a few hours to firm up.

4 Once firm, turn the cake onto your work surface and remove the baking paper. Slice into 16 squares. Serve.

~ **Makes 16** ~

Of chocolate mice and men

These chocolates are reminiscent of the penny sweets I ate in childhood. I've made the chocolates using mice moulds and mini gingerbread men moulds – hence the name of the recipe. You can use flavourings and colourings of your choice (just keep an eye out for your e-numbers, especially E120; it is not vegan), as well as your choice of mould.

300g vegan white chocolate, broken into pieces
¼ teaspoon peppermint essence
¼ teaspoon green food colouring
¼ teaspoon coconut essence
¼ teaspoon lemon essence
¼ teaspoon yellow food colouring

1 Place the white chocolate in a bowl over a saucepan of simmering water. Melt gently over a low heat, stirring until smooth. Remove from the heat. Divide the chocolate between 3 small bowls.

2 To the first bowl, add the peppermint essence and green food colouring. Mix thoroughly to combine the colours and flavouring. Use a teaspoon to fill your moulds.

3 To the second bowl, add the coconut essence, stirring thoroughly. Spoon into the moulds.

4 To the final bowl, add the lemon essence and yellow food colouring. Stir well then fill your moulds.

5 Leave the chocolates to set firmly before removing them from the moulds. Serve.

~ Makes 15 ~

Treacle tarts

Treacle tarts are really simple to make. I have made the process even faster by using ready-made pastry cases. Feel free to use your own pastry recipe if you have the time, but you will need to blind bake the pastry first. See cook's notes for instructions.

12 pre-cooked pastry cases
150g golden syrup
1 cup / 60g fresh white bread crumbs
Grated peel and juice of 1 lemon

Preheat the oven to 180°C / 350°F / Gas Mark 4

1 Place the pastry cases on a baking tray.

2 Pour the golden syrup into a small saucepan then heat over a low heat for 3 minutes. Stir in the bread crumbs, lemon peel and juice. Make sure the bread crumbs are coated in the syrup. Spoon the mixture into the pastry cases. Bake for 30 minutes, until golden and set. Serve warm or cold.

~ Makes 12 ~

Chocolate brownies

What's there to say about the fantastic brownie? Easy to prepare and heavenly to eat. You can serve these to your guests warm or cold.

1 cup / 150g plain flour
1 teaspoon baking powder
½ teaspoon salt
1 cup / 75g cocoa powder
1 cup / 200g caster sugar
100g vegan margarine
½ cup / 125ml water
1 teaspoon vanilla extract

Preheat the oven to 180°C / 350°F / Gas Mark 4

1 Sift the flour, baking powder and salt into a bowl.

2 Place the cocoa powder, sugar, margarine and water in a medium saucepan. Place over a low heat and stir until the mixture is melted and smooth. Remove from the heat. Stir in the flour, mixing well.

3 Pour the mixture into a greased and lined 20cm square baking tin and bake for 25 minutes, until firm on top. Let stand in the tin to cool, before removing and discarding the baking paper. Slice into 16 squares then serve.

~ **Makes 16** ~

Pecan and date fudge

Using sweetened condensed soy milk for this fudge recipe means it is quick to make and you do not need a sugar thermometer. If you do not like pecans, substitute with your choice of chopped nut. You may like to serve the fudge at the end of the evening, with coffee.

320g can condensed soy milk
1½ cups / 225g dark chocolate, broken into pieces
½ cup / 60g pecans, chopped
½ cup / 70g dried dates, chopped
1 tablespoon maple syrup

1 Pour the condensed soy milk into a small saucepan. Add the chocolate. Heat over a low heat, stirring occasionally with a wooden spoon. You want the chocolate to be melted and the mixture to be smooth. This will take about 5 minutes. Remove from the heat.

2 Stir in the pecans, chopped dates and maple syrup. Pour into a 20cm square tin, lined with baking paper. Leave to cool for 30 minutes before placing in the refrigerator to firm up for at least 2 hours.

3 Once the fudge is firm, remove from the tin and discard the baking paper. Use a large sharp knife to cut the fudge into bite-size pieces. Serve.

~ Makes 36 ~

Shortbread

Like roast potatoes, shortbread should be kept simple. I have added vanilla extract, but have resisted the urge to add extra flavourings so you can enjoy this sweet treat at its best.

1 cup / 150g plain flour
½ cup / 75g rice flour
Pinch of salt
½ cup / 100g caster sugar
200g vegan margarine
1 teaspoon vanilla extract
1 tablespoon caster sugar, for dusting

Preheat the oven to 160°C / 325°F / Gas Mark 3

1 Sift the flours and salt into a food processor. Add the sugar, margarine and vanilla extract. Process until a ball of dough forms.

2 Press the dough firmly into a greased and lined 20cm square tin. Use the back of a spoon to flatten it out. Prick all over with a fork. Bake in the oven for 35-40 minutes, until pale golden brown. Remove from the oven and cut into 16 squares whilst it is still hot. Dust with caster sugar. Leave to cool in the tin before transferring to a serving plate. Serve.

~ **Makes 16** ~

Raspberry and chocolate cheesecakes

If you are a fan of pink, you will adore these cheesecakes. Raspberries are crushed into the cream cheese mixture, giving them their gorgeous colour. You can make these at any time of year as frozen raspberries are used.

1½ cups / 150g frozen raspberries
1 tablespoon caster sugar
180g digestive / wheatmeal biscuits
90g vegan margarine
½ cup / 80g vegan white chocolate, broken into pieces
250g vegan cream cheese
¼ cup / 60ml coconut cream
¼ cup / 40g vegan white chocolate, grated

1 In a small saucepan add the raspberries and caster sugar. Heat over a low heat for 5 minutes, crushing the raspberries with the back of a spoon as you do so. Remove from the heat and leave to cool.

2 Place the biscuits in a plastic bag and beat to a crumb with a rolling pin (alternatively you can process them in a food processor, but beating is more fun). Melt the margarine over a low heat in a medium saucepan. Once melted, remove from the heat and add the crushed biscuits. Stir well. Line a 12-hole muffin tin with muffin cases and spoon the biscuit mixture evenly between the cases. Press down firmly with the back of a metal spoon.

3 Place the white chocolate in a bowl over a saucepan of simmering water. Melt gently over a low heat, stirring until smooth.

4 In a large bowl, beat together the cream cheese and coconut cream, using electric beaters. Stir in the raspberries and melted white chocolate. Spoon the mixture evenly over the biscuit base. Sprinkle on the grated chocolate. Place in the refrigerator for 2 hours. Remove the cheesecakes from the muffin tin. Serve.

~ Makes 12 ~

Smiley Rileys

Sweet biscuits sandwiched together with a jammy-creamy filling; what could be better? When the biscuits have a smiley face on them. I used smiley face cookie cutters that I picked up on a recent trip to the UK. If you cannot get hold of them, regular cutters will do fine. You will just have Rileys.

225g vegan margarine
⅔ cup / 125g caster sugar
1 teaspoon vanilla extract
2⅓ cups/ 350g self-raising flour
Pinch of salt

For the filling:
100g vegan margarine
2 tablespoons soy milk
1 teaspoon vanilla extract
2 cups / 250g icing sugar
½ cup / 160g raspberry jam

Preheat the oven to 180°C / 350°F / Gas Mark 4

1 In a food processor or large bowl, beat together the margarine and caster sugar. Mix in the vanilla extract. Add the flour and a pinch of salt. Process or beat until the mixture forms a dough. Cover in plastic wrap then refrigerate for 30 minutes.

2 Using a floured rolling pin, roll out the dough until it is about 5mm thick. Cut out your biscuits and place on a lined baking tray, leaving room for spreading. You will need 2 large trays. Bake in the oven for 12-15 minutes, until lightly golden and puffed. Let stand for 10 minutes before transferring to a wire rack to cool. Cool completely before adding the filling.

3 To make the filling, beat the margarine until it is very soft. Beat in the milk and vanilla extract. Add the icing sugar and continue beating until the mixture is pale, light and fluffy.

4 Prepare the jam by placing in a bowl and giving it a good stir to make it easier to handle.

5 To finish your biscuits, spread a teaspoon of the cream filling onto each biscuit, add a teaspoon of jam and top with another biscuit. Arrange on a serving plate. Serve.

~ **Makes 24** ~

Fruits with chocolate dip

The healthy way to eat chocolate! A platter of fruit, served with chocolate dip makes a colourful and flavoursome dessert. I have offered fruit suggestions; choose your favourites or what's in season. Aim for a variety of colours and make sure the fruit is in bite-size pieces.

Strawberries, kept whole
Raspberries, kept whole
Grapes, kept whole
Oranges, segmented
Mandarins, segmented
Kiwi fruit, peeled and quartered
Banana, sliced into chunks
Apple, sliced into segments

For the chocolate dip:
150g dark chocolate, broken into pieces
⅔ cup / 160ml coconut cream
½ teaspoon vanilla extract
½ teaspoon ground cinnamon

1 Prepare your choice of fruits and arrange on a platter. Be careful preparing apple and banana too early as they will brown.

2 To make the chocolate dip, combine the chocolate and coconut cream in a small saucepan over a medium heat. Stir the mixture until it is melted and combined. Remove from the heat and stir in the vanilla extract and cinnamon. Pour the dip into a serving bowl and serve with the fruit.

~ Makes just under 1 cup chocolate dip ~

Churros with chocolate dip

Churros are Spanish doughnuts perfect for an end of evening treat. The chocolate dip contains salt and chilli; if you prefer, use the chocolate dip recipe on the previous page. You will need a large star-shaped nozzle and disposable piping bag to make the churros.

1 tablespoon golden flaxmeal
3 tablespoons warm water
125g vegan margarine
1 cup / 250ml water
1⅓ cup / 200g plain flour
Pinch of salt
Canola oil, for deep-frying
Granulated / vanilla sugar, for dredging

For the chocolate dip:
150g dark chocolate, broken into pieces
⅔ cup / 160ml coconut cream
½ teaspoon salt
¼ teaspoon chilli powder

1 Place the flaxmeal and 3 tablespoons of warm water in a food processor and blitz until combined and thick. Leave to stand for 10 minutes.

2 In a medium saucepan, bring the margarine and water to the boil. Reduce the heat to low, then using a wooden spoon, beat in the flour and salt. It will come away from the pan and will only take a few seconds. Finally, beat in the flaxmeal mixture, mixing thoroughly.

3 Fill a large saucepan with canola oil until it is ⅓ full. Attach a thermometer to the pan then heat the oil over a medium heat until it reaches 190°C / 375°F.

4 While the oil is heating, stand your piping bag with nozzle attached in a jug. Fold down the top of the bag and spoon some of the doughnut mixture in. Only half-fill the bag. Twist the top.

5 Once the oil is ready, hold the bag over the pan using your non-dominant hand. Squeeze out about 6cm of mixture and using scissors in your other hand, cut the mixture and let it drop into the oil. You can add about 10 at a time, but you may

need to move them about to stop them from sticking to each other. Fry for about 1 minute, until they are golden. Remove with a slotted spoon and drain on paper towel. Transfer to a bowl and dredge with sugar. Repeat for the rest of the mixture, making sure the oil gets back up to temperature before adding more.

6 To make the chocolate dip, combine the chocolate and coconut cream in a small saucepan over a medium heat. Stir the mixture until it is melted and combined. Remove from the heat and stir in the salt and chilli powder. Pour the dip into a serving bowl and serve with the churros.

~ **Makes about 50 churros and 1 cup chocolate dip** ~

Lemon tarts

I used ready-prepared pastry cases to make this recipe even easier. Do use your own pastry recipe if you prefer, but remember you will need to blind bake the pastry first. See cook's notes for instructions.

200g firm tofu, crumbled
¼ cup / 50g caster sugar
Finely grated peel and juice of 2 lemons
12 pre-cooked pastry cases

1 Place the tofu, caster sugar, lemon peel and juice in a food processor. Process until creamy and smooth.

2 Fill the pastry shells with the lemon mixture. Place in the fridge for a couple of hours to firm up. Serve.

~ **Makes 12** ~

Index

D

E

26695977R00107

Made in the USA
Middletown, DE
05 December 2015